Contents

Introduction

There is today a growing and keen interest in all aspects of furnishing the home. This interest is not confined to purchasing ready-made items, or seeking professional services. Many people are now making or remaking household furnishings and furniture themselves with a high degree of success.

Standards of workmanship and the design of articles made at home can at least equal and are often superior to those sold in shops. The amateur does not count the cost of his time and so can afford to take time searching for materials, work slowly if necessary and take time to correct any imperfections.

Success is not automatic, but advice and inspiration are available from many sources. Courses in local colleges, television programmes and reference books all provide ideas and good instruction. It is very important to think and plan before plunging into a new project or before indulging in a shopping spree to buy new materials. There is a variety of factors to be considered: where the material is to be used, the aspect of the room, the amount of wear it will have, and how it will blend with other furnishings in the room.

The techniques and approach to all types of furnishings have undergone major changes in recent years. Changes in the style and sizes of windows have caused manufacturers to produce fabrics of greater widths; 80 cm (31 in) fabric has almost disappeared and 120 cm (48 in) is now the commonest width. Some fabrics are produced up to 2.5 m (8 ft 6 in) wide today, so that now the fabric width becomes the drop of the curtain. The increased variety of headings now available widens the choice of finishes at the top of the curtain.

The more widespread use of central heating and double glazing has reduced the importance of curtains for retaining heat and excluding draughts. Generally higher living temperatures have also extended the range of colours which can be used in north- or east-facing rooms or for covering lampshades. Warm colours were previously used to give an illusion of warmth; now, blues and greens are popular.

Modern sewing machines can make light of many sewing chores. Blind hemming attachments make it possible to produce curtains of the same quality as those previously made by hand. Other attachments and discs can be used to decorate cushions, duvet covers and household linens as well as to neaten all seams securely.

Perhaps the most important change has been the production and ready availability of 'easy-care' fabrics. With the rising cost of professional cleaning, the use of furnishing fabrics that can be washed at home is an important consideration. Although these fabrics solve many problems, each has its own peculiar hazard and the washing instructions for each must be carefully followed. Some fabrics made from man-made fibres can be ruined by over-heated water, over-soaking or over-spinning. When exposed to such conditions they become permanently creased and lose their immaculate appearance. Drip-drying is often a good method of treating these fabrics; if they are spin-dried, it should be for the shortest time. It is important to know the composition of each fabric; this information can be obtained from the shop when you buy the material.

The satisfaction derived from creating a home of beauty is ample reward for the work and patience involved. It is no longer necessary to spend large sums of money on furnishings to produce beautiful and comfortable results. Today, the successful home is the one which reflects its owner's personality.

HOME CRAFTS

Dorothy Cox

Consultant: Pat Cherry
NFWI Home Economics Adviser

Macdonald Educational in association with WI Books Ltd.

Metric Conversion Table

Fabric Widths

Imperial	Metric
35-36 in	90 cm
44-45 in	1 m 15 cm
48 in	1 m 20 cm
54-56 in	1 m 40 cm
60 in	1.5 m

Fabrics measured in metric lengths are sold to the nearest 10 cm.
The widths have not been altered, although now expressed in metric terms.

Upholstery Materials

Foam

Imperial	Metric
1 in	25 mm
2 in	50 mm
3 in	75 mm

Tacks

Imperial	Metric
$\frac{3}{8}$ in	10 mm
$\frac{1}{2}$ in	12 mm
$\frac{5}{8}$ in	15 mm

Webbing

Imperial	Metric
1 in	25 mm
$1\frac{1}{2}$ in	37 mm
2 in	50 mm

Designed and created by
Berkeley Publishers Ltd.
9 Warwick Court
London WC1R 5DJ

Editor John Axon
Design Peter Davies and Peter Green

Photography Peter Myers
Fabrics from Fabric International, Derby

Illustrations Fiona Almeleh, Rene Eyre and David Parr

© WI Books Ltd. 1978

First published 1978
Macdonald Educational Ltd.
Holywell House
Worship Street
London EC2A 2EN

Editorial manager
Chester Fisher
Publishing co-ordinator
Gill Rowley
Production managers
Eva Wrennall and Penny Kitchenham

Made and printed by
Purnell & Sons Ltd.,
Paulton

ISBN 0 356 06128 0

Acknowledgements

The publishers would like to thank the following for kindly loaning items for the photographs in this book:

Fabric International, Derby
Robinsons Decorators, Derby
U-do-it, Ripley, Derby
and members of the Derbyshire Federation of Women's Institutes for loaning examples of their work

A tack in time...

Many people who have discovered how difficult it is to find a craftsman to repair
a treasured piece of furniture have accepted the challenge of do-it-yourself
upholstery, and this has given rise to a great awakening of interest in traditional
methods and materials. But you may also here discover the pleasure to be gained
from learning modern techniques and the use of new materials, from which can be
created something quite new.

Upholstery–Modern and Traditional

Upholstery is a very practical craft indeed. Although it can be traced back several centuries to very early origins, a whole range of new materials has appeared over the last few decades which has—in some people's opinions—invalidated the old techniques. As both traditional and modern materials have their devotees, instructions for using both are given here.

A complete newcomer to upholstery will probably find the new materials—together with the new techniques they require—easier to use. Your main aim, whichever you prefer, should be to work towards highly professional results, in terms of both appearance and longevity.

Materials and Equipment for Traditional Upholstery

Traditional webbing

This is made from jute, linen or cotton or a combination of these fibres. The best quality is the black and white linen webbing with a twill weave. Though the fawn webbing with a plain weave is the cheapest, it also tends to stretch and will eventually break. As the webbing forms the foundation of any upholstery (so, to a large extent, determining the life of a seat), use the best quality obtainable.

Stuffings

These vary in availability, resilience, length of life and cost. The most highly sought after is animal hair from the horse, goat or pig. Its quality and resilience is determined by the length and the curl of each hair. The shorter the hair, the less the curl, which reduces the resilience accordingly and makes for a less comfortable piece of upholstery. Hair is in short supply today. Much of that in use has been reclaimed from stripped down furniture. Old hair thus obtained can be washed in good detergent but must always be rinsed well and dried very thoroughly. Hair is frequently combined with rubber latex to produce rubberized hair. This has an open texture and, made in sheet form, can be used as solid sheet foam.

Cheaper fillings are made from vegetable fibres, the commonest being the brown coco or coir fibre. The disadvantage of this type of stuffing is that it eventually breaks up into short pieces and finally turns to dust, causing the upholstery to lose both shape and comfort.

Wadding and Lintafelt

These materials are used to cover the hair or coir stuffings. The nature of these materials prevents the fibres penetrating through the outer cover, which would prove uncomfortable for the user. Lintafelt is much coarser and thicker than sheet wadding, is used on larger pieces of work and can also be teased and used for buttoning.

Hessian, scrim, calico and lining

Hessian is a jute product made in a variety of weights and densities but to an average width of 200 cm (72 in). It has various uses in uphol-

Traditional upholstery materials: . webbing over natural hessian

2

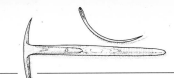

stery, such as covering the webbing or springs or even forming the foundation of the back of a small chair where it is impossible to use webbing. It should be very strong and closely woven.

Scrim is very similar to hessian but it is made from a finer fibre and much more loosely woven. It is used to cover the first stuffing (especially when this stuffing has to be stitched up) so as to form a firm edge or roll for the upholstery.

Unbleached calico is both stronger and cheaper than the bleached fabric. It is frequently used both to cover the final stuffing and as an undercover. Use lightweight quality to avoid bulk, particularly on drop-in seats and at corners.

Black linen lining is a closely woven fabric used to finish the underside of seats. As it is very expensive, a closely woven hessian may be used instead.

Twines

These are used for a number of different processes, so are made in a variety of thicknesses. The strength of twine is very important. Traditional upholstery twines are made from flax. There are also some good nylon twines on the market which are cheaper and can be used without loss of strength, but do not use cheap string, which is too weak. The twine used for lashing springs into position is often referred to as 'laid-cord'.

Tacks

It is essential to use only proper upholstery tacks. They are usually blue in colour and always very sharp. They have been specially designed for their purpose; they start to taper from the head and end in a needle-sharp point so that they stay in position when pressed lightly into a wooden frame. They therefore prevent painful, hammered fingers!

Preparing for action: getting tools and materials together

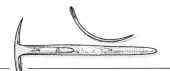

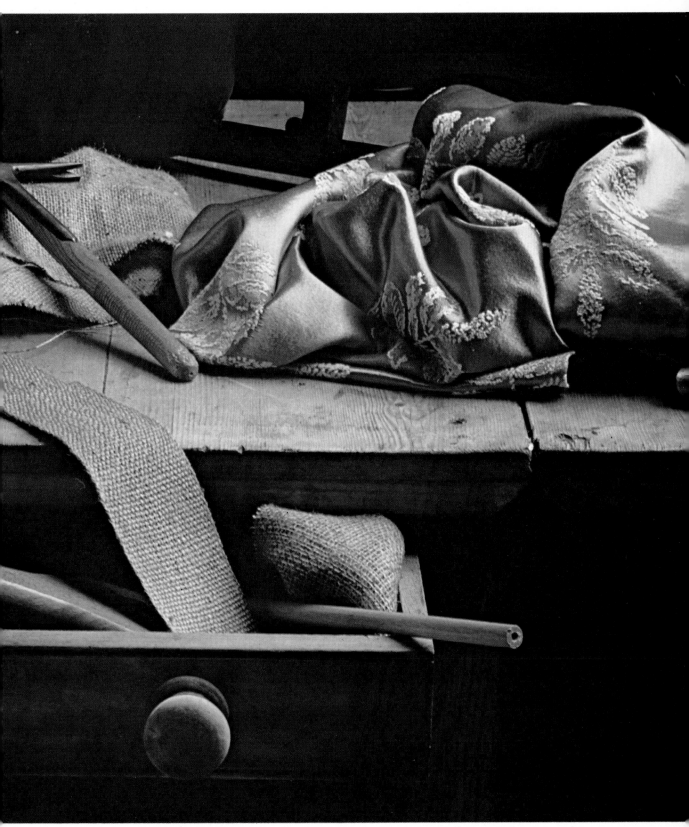

The various tacks available suit specific purposes:

15-mm ($\frac{5}{8}$-in) 'Improved' tacks These are designed to attach the webbing to the frame. 'Improved' means that the tack has a large head which will sit on the webbing and not cut into or through it.

13- or 10-mm ($\frac{1}{2}$- or $\frac{3}{8}$-in) 'Improved' tacks These are best used for small or delicate pieces of furniture where thicker tacks might split the frame.

10-mm ($\frac{3}{8}$-in) fine tacks These are for general upholstery purposes, such as attaching materials to the frame. They have a smaller head and are generally altogether finer than the larger tacks. If you need to anchor very thick fabric or several layers of material, use 13-mm ($\frac{1}{2}$-in) fine tacks rather than these very small ones.

Gimp pins These are available in many colours and are very fine and sharp with tiny heads. Use them to fix gimp into position.

Stool, sewing chair, prayer chair: the chairs have sprung seats covered by hair and wadding, the stool is also upholstered-over

Tools

Hammer A good hammer is essential. Upholstery hammers may have two driving surfaces of different sizes or one driving surface with a claw for removing tacks at the other end. To get the maximum effect with the minimum effort, hold the hammer at the end of the handle and then use it with a loose wrist action. To remove tacks, turn the hammer sideways to hit the end of the stripping chisel (see below). This will save you buying a wooden mallet.

If you find it difficult to obtain an upholstery hammer, use a well-balanced hammer with a small head (approximately 13 mm/½ in), at least for the first piece of upholstery you undertake. Eventually, however, an upholstery hammer will prove a good investment.

Stripping chisel This is used to remove tacks, from both old upholstery, when it is being stripped, and new upholstery, when the tack is driven into the frame askew. Hold the sharp end of the chisel at an angle to the head of the tack and hit with hammer or mallet.

Tack-lifter This is an optional piece of equipment for removing tacks. It is shaped like a chisel, but has a slightly curved end which

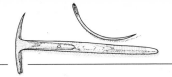

is divided, resembling a claw.
Web-stretcher If using traditional webbing, this is an essential piece of equipment for ensuring that the webbing is pulled taut to give a firm base to the subsequent stuffing. Stretchers vary in design, but the most common is a shaped piece of wood with a groove at one end. There is a slot in the wood through which the folded webbing is inserted. This is then held securely with a small piece of dowelling placed through the fold of the webbing (figure 2). With practice, a block of wood 15 x 8 cm (6 x 3 in) and 1-2 cm ($\frac{1}{2}$-$\frac{3}{4}$ in) thick can be used.

Needles and regulator You will need various types of needle for different stages.

A mattress needle is pointed at both ends and may vary in length from 20-30 cm (8-14 in). It is used to stitch through stuffing and for buttoning.

A bayonet needle is similar to a mattress needle except that the end with the eye is rounded and the other end is triangular. It is used to stitch up rolls or edges.

A spring needle resembles a large darning or packing needle and is slightly curved at the pointed end. It is used for stitching springs into position.

Semi-circular needles are made in various sizes and are used for stitching fabrics together in difficult places, e.g. attaching the outside back to a chair or securing pleats on the front corners of a chair.

*(Left) Some of the upholstery tools you may need when using either traditional or modern methods:
(top row) normal stripping chisel, adjustable bladed Stanley knife;
(2nd row) narrow stripping chisel, tack with magnetic central pin;
(3rd row) curved stripping knife;
(4th row) dowelling for use with web stretcher, needles, small tack, upholsterer's hammer, web stretcher;
(bottom row) stripping mallet*

A regulator, as its name suggests, is used to regulate the thickness, quantity and evenness of the stuffing. Insert the pointed end through the scrim to regulate or remove any unevenness in the first stuffing or when stitching up a roll or edge.

Fine metal skewers are useful for holding fabrics in position prior to stitching or sewing.

Springs

The two most common types available are the coil spring and the tension spring.

Coil springs vary from 10 to 25 cm (4 to 10 in) in height and from 13-gauge (thin) to 8-gauge (thick). Smaller and more delicate springs are used for proportionally small pieces of furniture and the backs and arms of chairs. Larger seats obviously need larger and stronger springs.

Tension springs are suitable for chairs which have a loose cushion placed on the seat. They are closely coiled, usually covered in plastic, with a hook at each end. These hooks fasten into metal strips or rings located on the sides of the chair.

Materials and Equipment for Modern Upholstery

Pirelli webbing

This is a comparatively new type of webbing. It is very easy to use and has a very long life provided it is screened from the light by a closely woven lining. Easy for the amateur or beginner to handle, it is also suitable for replacing springs. This is an advantage when springs wear through the covering spring hessian, resulting in 'floating' springs which are very uncomfortable to sit on.

Pirelli webbing is made of strips of material cut on the cross and impregnated with rubber, and can

be stretched or tensioned to produce a firm but elastic base on which to build the rest of the seat. It is produced in several widths but you will find webbing that is 38 or 50 mm ($1\frac{1}{2}$ or 2 in) wide most useful.

Foam

Two types are produced: latex foam, which is made largely from the latex of the rubber tree, and polyurethane foam, which is a synthetic material.

Latex foam is manufactured by introducing gas into latex while it is in a semi-liquid form. It is this aeration which gives the foam its characteristic texture, and the volume of air or gas introduced determines its density and comfort. For seats, a foam of 'medium firm' density gives the most comfortable result, but for backs and arms of chairs, choose a less firm foam.

One very important advantage of latex foam is that it has 100 per cent recovery properties: however many times it is compressed when sat on (if used for seating purposes), it will spring back to its original shape. It is more expensive than synthetic foam but is well worth the extra money. Its other virtues are that it is moth-, mildew- and germ-proof, and is easy to handle and shape. However, it will *not* tolerate exposure to light. This makes it perish and crumble.

There are two forms of latex foam: plain sheeting and pin core. Each has a particular use. Plain sheeting is made 13 and 25 mm ($\frac{1}{2}$ and 1 in) thick. Use the thicker of these for re-upholstering 'drop-in' seats and 'pin-cushion' seats. (For both these seats it is essential to have adequate rubber, without great depth of foam, which would spoil the design of the chair seat.)

Pin core foam has thousands of circular holes, approximately 5 mm ($\frac{1}{4}$ in) in diameter, running through the material. This makes a given volume of the aerated latex fill a

Natural hessian neatens underside

larger volume and so reduces the cost of the foam. It is produced in various thicknesses but the most popular for domestic upholstery is 50 mm (2 in) thick. If you want a deeper seat, use more than one thickness, or incorporate a layer of polyurethane under the latex.

Polyurethane foam is used very widely today because it is less expensive to produce than latex.

It has, however, been the subject of considerable criticism as, in the past, it presented a high fire risk. As a result, certain manufacturers have researched the problem and are now able to produce a 'flame-resist' foam. It is important to ask for this quality when purchasing.

Polyurethane foam is made in a wide range of densities and firmness. Soft foams will not produce comfortable seats, but can be used with success for footstools, arms and backs of chairs, as underlayers on deep seats and for bedheads.

Calico, hessian and lining

As in traditional upholstery, use hessian or black linen lining for

neatening the underside of seats When choosing a lining to go under foam, it is particularly important to select one that is closely woven, so as to exclude light and thus prevent deterioration. A lightweight unbleached calico may be used both as an undercover and in strip form to attach the foam to the wooden frame.

Equipment

The hammers, chisels, tacks and needles (with the exception of spring needles) are the same as those used in traditional upholstery, but you will not need a web-stretcher or regulator. As Pirelli webbing is rubberized and elastic, springs are not necessary.

Adhesive

Whichever type of foam you are using, it must be joined to the base of the piece of furniture with strips of calico. These must be stuck to the foam with an adhesive. Use one suitable for latex and synthetic foams—it will become invisible and yet remain soft and pliable when dry. Use one of the special upholstery adhesives available. Apply the adhesive to both surfaces and allow to dry before joining them together. It is impossible to separate the layers once they have been placed together: if you apply force to

remove the calico, you will tear a layer of foam from the top .

Re-upholstering a Drop-in Seat (traditional method and materials)

Stripping the old frame

Begin by removing all the old upholstery—that is, the stuffing, hessian, webbing and tacks. Remove the tacks by holding the sharp end of a chisel or screwdriver at an angle to the head of each tack and hitting the opposite end sharply with the side of the hammer or a mallet. Strip the frame along the grain of the wood, which is usually parallel to the edge of the frame. You will find that hitting the chisel in this direction reduces the risk of splitting. If you strip at right angles to the edge (often easier) it is highly likely that you will knock out a piece of the frame.

Note This danger has increased greatly with the advent of central heating, which dries out wooden furniture frames.

When you have completed all the stripping, examine any weak joints carefully and, if necessary, reinforce and glue them. Treat any signs of woodworm with an injector and fill tack holes with plastic wood.

Before beginning the upholstery, consider the thickness of the new cover. This style of seat should fit

closely into the chair with no movement of the drop-in section. If you are using a cover fabric which is thinner than the original, then you may need to build up the sides of the frame with strips of cardboard to prevent a gap between the seat and the frame. Conversely, if the new cover fabric is thicker, which it may well be if you have worked a canvas for the new cover, you may need to plane the frame along the edges, otherwise the seat will sit *on* the chair instead of fitting *into* the frame. If you do not make these adjustments, should they be necessary, the newly upholstered seat may not fit into the chair. You would then have to strip it completely and start all over again.

Webbing the frame

Work with the champhered or bevelled side of the frame uppermost. When attaching the webbing, the space left between adjacent webs should not be greater than the width of the webbing itself. For an average drop-in seat, two to three webs are needed in each direction.

1. Mark the centre points of the back and front rails. Usually these seats are tapered, so the webs should be staggered so that they are slightly further apart at the front than at the back.

2. If using three webs, begin at the centre of the back rail. Fold over 3 cm (1 in) of the woven webbing and place the folded edge about 1 cm ($\frac{1}{2}$ in) in from the back edge of the frame. Attach with five 15-mm ($\frac{5}{8}$-in) improved tacks (figure 1).

3. Fix the webbing through or round the stretcher (figure 2), then bring it across the frame to the front edge. Or a block of wood can be used (figure 3). Lever the stretcher against the edge of the front rail (figure 4) until the webbing is very tight. Anchor with three improved tacks. Cut off the webbing, leaving a surplus of 3 cm (1 in). Turn this back and anchor

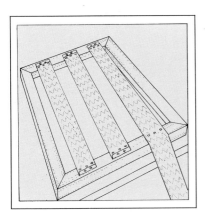

1 *Attach webbing with improved tacks*

2 *Feed webbing through stretcher*

with two more tacks. It is necessary to fold back the ends of woven webbing to prevent it fraying when under strain.

4. Attach the other webs, working from the back to the front of the frame and keeping them taut.

5. Weave in the cross webs to give a firm base (figure 5), stretching these as the vertical webs.

Attaching the hessian

6. Cut a piece of closely woven hessian to the size of the frame plus a seam allowance of 1 cm ($\frac{1}{2}$ in) all round, making sure you cut along the straight grain of the fabric. Turn in 1·5 cm ($\frac{3}{4}$ in) along the back edge and attach just inside

Detail of unchamfered drop-in frame, seen from above: it has been webbed with traditional materials, black and white linen webbing with a twill weave, and has been covered with a natural jute hessian

the edge of the back rail using 10-mm ($\frac{3}{8}$-in) fine tacks.

7. Bring the hessian to the front rail, pull it tightly and attach it 1 cm ($\frac{1}{2}$ in) from the front edge of the frame. Turn back the surplus material and anchor with a few 10-mm ($\frac{3}{8}$-in) fine tacks.

8. Insert a temporary tack in the middle of one side and tack the hessian to the opposite side rail as on

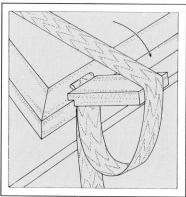

3 Bring webbing to front and insert block of wood

the front rail. Remove the temporary tack and, tightening against the side already tacked, finish attaching the hessian. (The hessian prevents the stuffing escaping through the webbing.)

Making the bridles

9. Using a curved needle and thread with stitching twine, pick up 1 cm

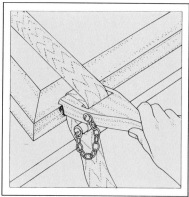

4 Lever stretcher against edge of front rail

*Dining room chair with drop-in seat;
the upholstery has been built on woven
webbing covered by hessian, fibre
filling has been secured by bridles and
covered by calico and wadding, with a
final cover of Dralon velvet*

13

Underside view of drop-in frame

($\frac{1}{2}$ in) of hessian at the back left-hand corner, draw the twine through and secure with a slip-knot. Pick up another 1 cm ($\frac{1}{2}$ in) of hessian half way along the back edge with the point of the needle facing the back left-hand corner, thus forming a back stitch. Follow this by another stitch in the back right-hand corner. Continue until you have stitched 'bridles' all round the edge of the hessian. Finally, work a 'cross' of bridles in the middle of the seat (figure 6).

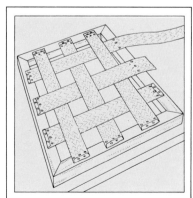

5 *Weave in cross webs, stretching as for vertical webs*

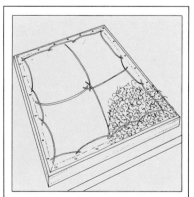

6 *Work a cross of bridles*

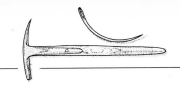

Inserting the stuffing

10. An average dining chair requires approximately 500 g (1 lb) of hair or fibre. Take a handful of stuffing and tease it thoroughly to remove any lumps. Place it under one of the back bridles. Repeat this process along the back edge, round the sides, and along the front edge. Then gradually fill up the centre of the chair, making the stuffing slightly thicker here than at the sides, to give a good shape to the finished seat. Pad the edges well to prevent the wooden frame wearing through the covering fabric, but take care that no stuffing goes over the edge of the frame or it will not fit back into the chair. Check that the bridles are tight, so that they will prevent the filling moving about when the seat is in use.

Covering the seat

11. Cut a piece of scrim or thin calico sufficiently large to cover the stuffing and to reach to the underside of the frame. Place over the fibre or hair. Turn the seat over so that the covered stuffing is on the surface of the table and the webbing is uppermost. Then, using 10-mm ($\frac{3}{8}$-in) fine tacks, and ensuring that the grain of the material runs along the edge of the frame, tack the fabric to the back rail on the underside of the frame. Place the tacks 1 cm ($\frac{1}{2}$ in) in from the edge of the frame and 2 cm ($\frac{3}{4}$ in) apart.

12. Smooth the fabric firmly over the stuffing and take to the underside of the front rail of the frame. Place a tack in the centre of the front rail. Working outwards from the middle of the front rail, and stroking the fabric firmly from the back to the front of the seat, complete the tacking to the front underside of the frame.

13. Place a tack in the centre of the left side rail, stroke the fabric to the right sail and tack in place.

Work from the centre of the rail towards the corners as before. Remove the temporary tack from the left-hand rail, then stroke the fabric against the right-hand side to complete the tacking of the undercover. The open texture of the material allows for the disposal of any fullness at the corners. Check that the stuffing is smooth and adjust with the regulator possibly.

14. Cut a piece of sheet wadding to fit over the seat, remembering it must *not* extend down the sides of the frame. If possible, use wadding

---

Detail of the underside of a drop-in seat showing one corner folded and tacked (as in figure 7) and pleated and trimmed (as in figure 8); a black linen lining has been tacked to the underside of the frame to neaten all cut edges

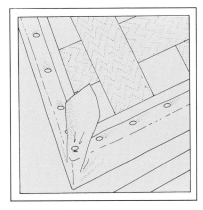

7 Insert tack in corner

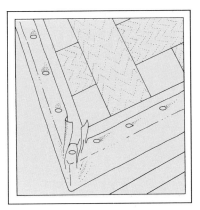

8 Fold and crease pleats, cut away surplus

with a thin skin as this will assist in preventing the fibres working through the top cover.

15. Choose the material or fabric for the top cover with care, bearing in mind the wear and friction it must withstand. It should be closely woven with no long threads which may pull. If using a vinyl material, choose one with a bonded jersey backing to prevent it splitting at the corners during tightening. When placing the material or fabric over the seat, centralize any motif or, if it has a striped design, make sure the stripes are straight and balanced. If there is a pile, this faces towards the front of the chair. Place a temporary tack in the centre of the underside of the back and front rails.

16. Tack the cover fabric along the back edge of the seat to within 5 cm (2 in) of the corners, inserting these tacks just inside the tacks fixing the undercover. Smooth the cover fabric towards the front of the frame and tack. Tack the sides as for the scrim but leave 5 cm (2 in) untacked either side of each of the corners.

Finishing the corners

17. Working with the underside of the frame uppermost, hold the corner point of the cover and tighten towards the centre of the frame. Smooth it over the corner and insert a fine tack not more than 1 cm ($\frac{1}{2}$ in) from the corner (figure 7).

18. Fold the fabric over the corner and crease the pleats (figure 8). Then open out the fabric and cut away the surplus trimming round the tack to within $\frac{1}{2}$ cm ($\frac{1}{4}$ in) of the folds of the fabric. Bring the fabric over from one edge, smooth and insert another tack by the side of the one that is holding the fabric at the corner. Join up to the rest of the tacks on this edge, then trim the fabric. Complete the other side of the corner in the same way. Finish the other three corners in the same way.

Note It is important to avoid bulk at all the corners.

Lining the seat

19. Cut the lining 2·5 cm (1 in) larger than the frame. Turn in 2 cm ($\frac{3}{4}$ in) all round and press. Mitre all four corners (figure 9). Using fine tacks, anchor the lining to the four corners of the frame, then tack along the back edge, tighten it to the front and tack, and finally complete the sides.

Dining and Occasional Chairs with Upholstered-over Seats (traditional method and materials)

This style of chair may have the upholstery taken down the side of of the frame to the underside of the seat. Or it may reach over the side of the frame and finish just above a polished wooden border.

The first stage is to strip and check the frame in the same way as for the drop-in seat. If there are no springs, attach the webbing to the upper surface of the frame and then build up the stuffing as described from stage 5 of re-upholstering the drop-in seat onwards.

Attaching webbing for springs

1. The webbing is to be attached to

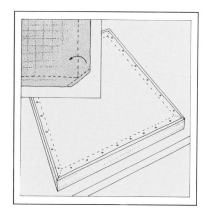

9 Mitre the corners

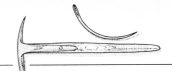

Dining chair with drop-in seat standing for comparison with newly upholstered-over sewing chair and stool with aligned stripe covers

the underside of the frame, so turn the chair upside down and rest the upper surface of the seat frame on a table. Attach the webbing as for a drop-in seat, increasing the number of webs if necessary. If using an even number of webs, there will be space down the centre, but this should not be wider than 3·5 cm (1½ in).

2. If you require a very firm seat, cover the webbing on the underside with a piece of hessian. Attach this in the same way as the lining on the drop-in seat.

3. Before placing and fixing the springs, decide how many you need. For an ordinary dining chair, allow three 15-cm (6-in) springs of 10-gauge wire (a carver may require five). These must be stitched to the webbing to prevent them moving during wear. Arrange the springs on top of the webbing and mark their positions (figure 10). Using strong twine and a spring needle and starting at the back of a spring, take the needle through from the underside of the webbing close to the bottom ring of the spring. Then take the needle over the wire and back through to the underside of the chair, securing it with a slip-knot. Move a quarter or one-third of the way round the spring and make a similar fastening, but anchor the thread with a half-hitch instead of a slip-knot. Repeat the process so that the spring is firmly anchored

in three or four places (figure 11). Finish the last tie with a double knot. Anchor the other springs in a similar way.

Lashing the springs

4. This process secures the springs in a slightly compressed state and increases the firmness of the seat. It is not necessary in very small chairs but it does tend to reduce the strain on the hessian.

Insert a 15-mm ($\frac{5}{8}$-in) improved tack to half its length on the top of the frame opposite the centre of each spring. Cut a length of laid-cord or lashing twine one and a half to two times the width of the frame. Twist the twine round the tack, and then drive the tack home. Take the cord to the outside of the slightly compressed spring and loop it around the wire (figure 12).

Take the cord to the opposite side of the spring and make a similar knot. Work across the springs and fasten the end of the twine to the opposite side of the frame with another tack. The correct compression of the springs will give an initial shaping to the seat. They are lashed to both sides and to the back and front of the seat.

Attaching the hessian

5. The springs must now be covered with hessian on which the rest of

the stuffing is built up. Working along the grain, cut a piece of fabric large enough to cover the seat plus a seam allowance of 2·5 cm (1 in). Turn in the 2·5-cm (1-in) allowance and tack the back of the hessian to the top of the back rail of the seat. Draw the fabric firmly towards the front rail and tack. Roll back the excess fabric and secure it. Tack the sides in the same way, then stitch the top of the springs to the hessian in the same way as the lower rings were stitched to the webbing.

Working the bridles

6. Using stitching twine, work a series of bridles as on the drop-in seat (stage 9). Insert the first stuffing under the bridles. Tease it well and cover the springs so that you can only just feel them through the stuffing. The surface of the seat should be flat, which means that the layer of stuffing is thicker around the edges of the chair than in the middle.

Stitching through

7. Cover the hair or fibre with a piece of scrim cut straight on the grain. Secure it with a few temporary tacks driven into the vertical side of the chair frame, so that the stuffing is held firmly. Stitch the seat by threading a mattress needle with a length of stitching twine and

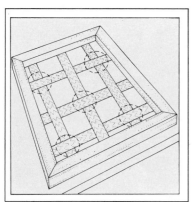

10 Mark position of springs on webbing

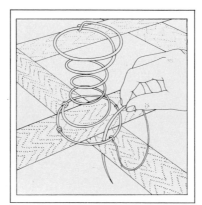

11 Anchor springs on webbing

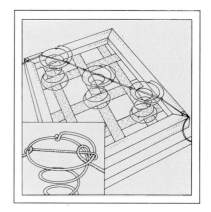

12 Loop cord around springs

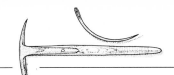

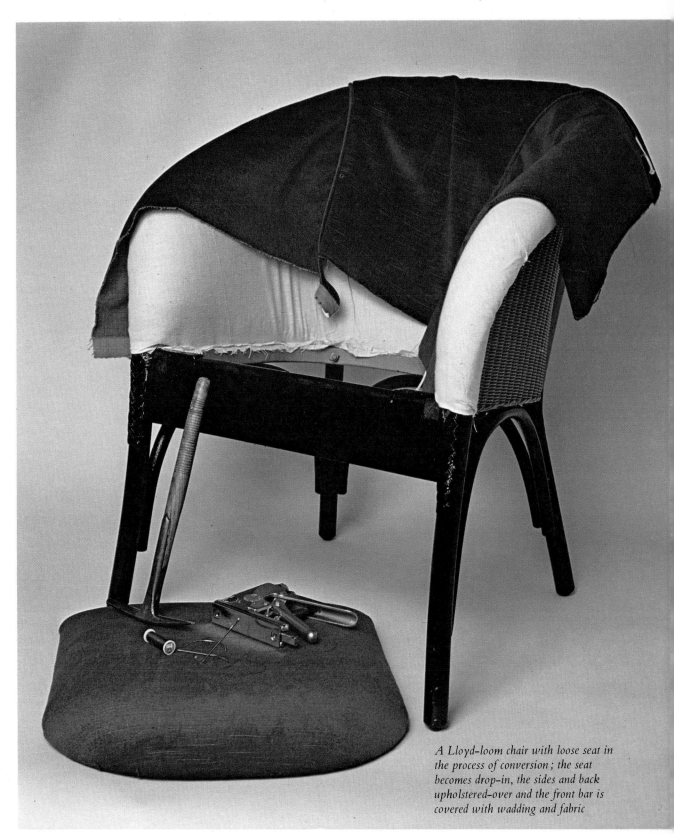

*A Lloyd-loom chair with loose seat in
the process of conversion; the seat
becomes drop-in, the sides and back
upholstered-over and the front bar is
covered with wadding and fabric*

Dining chair that is between styles of drop-in and upholstered-over; the removable seat is attached to the chair by wooden pegs

Sewing chair with upholstered-over seat; the striped cover has been aligned

pushing it right through the seat 8-10 cm (3-4 in) from the back left-hand corner, and returning it from the underside of the seat to about 2·5 cm (1 in) from where it first entered the stuffing. Secure with a slip-knot. Take the needle along the back edge, keeping the thread parallel with the edge of the frame, and work a similar stitch. No slip-knot is necessary at this point. Work all round the chair in this way (figure 13).

Tacking the scrim

8. Remove the temporary tacks and smooth the scrim away from the stitching firmly towards the frame of the chair. Re-tack, adding more stuffing if necessary to obtain a square and firm edge. Use the regulator as required to assist in this.

Blind- and top-stitching

9. These are two of the most important and skilled processes in upholstery and will need some practice. As there is a considerable

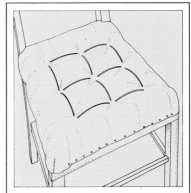

13 Secure stuffing with stitches

amount of stuffing around the edges it must be held rigidly in position if the upholstery is to retain a trim and firm appearance. To achieve this, work one row of blind-stitching and one or two rows, depending on the thickness, of top-stitching.

Begin the blind-stitching on the left side just in front of the back leg (figure 14). Thread a bayonet needle with stitching twine and anchor with a slip knot near the chair leg. Insert the bayonet end of the needle into the stuffing at an angle of 45° and draw it through the scrim until the eye is just visible, then push it back so that it emerges level with the point—but about 1 cm ($\frac{1}{2}$ in) behind where it was first inserted (figure 15). Before drawing the needle out of the stuffing, twist the twine around the needle, pull out the needle and draw the twine up very tightly (figure 16). Move on 5 cm (2 in) and repeat the stitch, taking care always to insert the needle at the same angle and the same distance.

Work all round the sides, front and back of the chair, securing the ends of the twine where necessary by wrapping it round a 10-mm ($\frac{3}{8}$-in) fine tack.

Begin the first row of top-stitching about 1 cm ($\frac{1}{2}$ in) above the previous row of blind-stitching (figure 17). Anchor the twine securely, then start stitching (figure 18). Draw the needle right through

the scrim and then re-insert it 2·5 cm (1 in) behind the point where it emerged, twisting the twine around the needle before with-drawing it at the lower level (figure 19). Use the regulator as necessary to keep the roll firm and even. Work a second row.

Top stuffing

10. Work another row of bridles round the top of the seat and then across the centre. Insert approximately 500 g (1 lb) of a good-quality fibre, hair if possible.

Attaching the covering

11. Cut a piece of wadding to fit over the hair and a piece of calico to cover this, then stretch down to the frame of the seat. Insert a temporary tack in the centre front and centre back of the seat frame. Tack the cover along the front edge just above the polished surround or underneath the frame, depending on the design of the chair. Remove the back temporary tack and smooth the material firmly towards the back of the chair. Place one tack at the centre back, followed by another 2 cm ($\frac{3}{4}$ in) to either side of this centre tack.

12. At the back corners, fold the fabric diagonally so that the fold just touches the upright. Slash the fabric at right angles to the fold to

within 1 cm ($\frac{1}{2}$ in) of the corner of the wood (figure 20). Draw the fabric around the wood and trim to 1 cm ($\frac{1}{2}$ in). Turn in this 1-cm ($\frac{1}{2}$-in) allowance and complete the tacking along the back. Smooth outwards from the centre, then tack both sides. Slash the fabric to the end of any fullness at the front corners. Overlap the two flaps and complete the tacking around the corners.

Note In this way, you will avoid creating a pleat at each corner in the undercover. This reduces bulk.

14. Attach the top cover in the same way as a drop-in seat, centralizing any pattern or stripes and working to within 5 cm (2 in) of the front corners when attaching the front edge. Complete the back edge, keeping the fabric tight around the back uprights. After tacking the sides, bring the fabric firmly around to the front edge and fold the front material downwards to form a pleat. Press the pleat and then lift and trim away to within 1 cm ($\frac{1}{2}$ in) of the folds (figure 21). Complete the tacking along the front edge and trim away any surplus fabric. If there is a polished surround to the chair, neaten the raw edges with a matching gimp attached with gimp-pins.

15. Cut and attach a lining to the underside of the chair as described for drop-in seat.

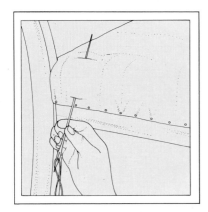

14 *Begin blind stitching near back left leg*

15 *Push needle back*

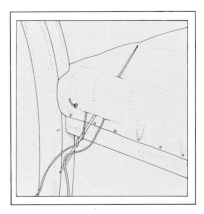

16 *Twist twine round needle*

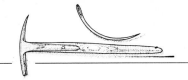

Detail of front corner of the stool shown earlier in the colour group; it is an upholstered-over stool with polished wood surround and the pleat of the tailored corner faces away from the centre front

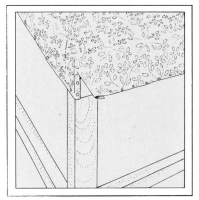

21 *Pleat front corner, trim away surplus*

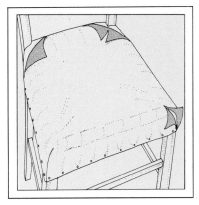

20 *Fold corners diagonally, slash at right angles*

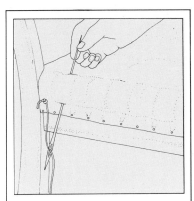

17 *Begin top stitching and anchor twine*

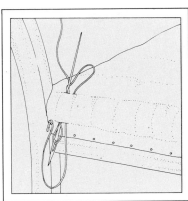

18 *Re-insert needle*

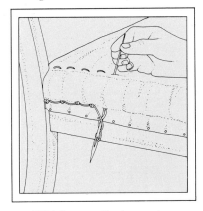

19 *Withdraw needle, knot twine*

Pin-cushion Seats (traditional method and materials)

This type of seat is one of the simplest forms of upholstery but it needs a great deal of care and also precision to get really professional results. It is often used for piano stools and delicate dining and bedroom chairs. The upholstered area does not lift out of the chair as it does with a drop-in seat but is set permanently into the centre of a seat surrounded by a polished wooden border. Inside the polished area there is a narrow border, usually rebated, to which all the upholstery is attached. Take great care, both while removing the old upholstery and attaching the new, not to split this narrow piece of wood. Protect the polished border with a piece of soft fabric during stripping and webbing.

Re-upholstering the seat

1. Web the seat using the same method as the drop-in seat, but use 10-mm ($\frac{3}{8}$-in) improved tacks instead of 15-mm ($\frac{5}{8}$-in) ones. (The larger tacks would be much too coarse to use on such a narrow and fragile border of wood.)
2. Cover the webbing with hessian and work the bridle ties as before (figure 23). Then upholster the seat

(Left) This prayer chair has an upholstered-over seat but the back has been upholstered in pin-cushion style, with the trimmed velvet neatened by a scroll gimp

(Above) Detail of back of prayer chair upholstered in pin-cushion style, showing ease and neatness of finishing off and cornering using scroll gimp which is joined at lower corner

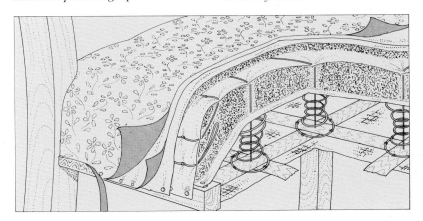

22 Cross-section of upholstered-over chair showing various stages

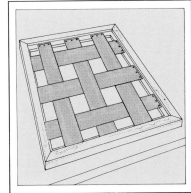

23 Webbing for pin cushion seat

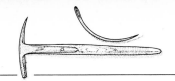

in exactly the same way as the drop-in seat but with all the tacks on the top of the frame. Cut away all the excess fabric with either a pair of fine scissors or a sharp knife. (Before doing so, reduce the risk of fraying by spreading a very narrow band of adhesive where the material is to be cut. Allow this to dry before cutting and trimming.)

Trimming the cut edge

3. Use a gimp with woven fabrics, banding with vinyl or leather covers or closely spaced domed nails. If using scroll gimp, you will find it very easy to take around corners and curves. Begin at one back corner using matching gimp pins every 2 cm (1 in). When fixing the end of the braid, seal it with a little adhesive to prevent fraying and turn under the first 1 cm ($\frac{1}{2}$ in).
4. To finish the gimping, seal and turn under the last 1 cm ($\frac{1}{2}$ in) and then join the two ends with a 'butt' join and secure with gimp pins.

The advantage of using scroll gimp is that the scrolls can be lifted and the pins inserted under the scrolls so that they cannot be seen on the finished seat. If it is impossible to obtain a matching gimp then use a braid and stick it in position with an upholstery adhesive or a clear adhesive. (It will not be possible to hide the gimp pins if using braid.) If using a clear adhesive, apply it to the gimp very thinly and work away from the chair to avoid the risk of dropping adhesive on the cover.
5. If you are neatening the cover with studs, the edges of the covering fabric should be turned in before close-nailing. Tack the cover temporarily into position, then trim

Bedroom chair with pin-cushion seat using traditional upholstery methods and materials; coir fibre and wadding were used as stuffing, the undercover was made of calico and the top cover was made of handworked canvas neatened with a border of scroll gimp

away the fabric to 1 cm ($\frac{1}{2}$ in). Remove the temporary tacks a few at a time, folding in the raw edges and anchoring the edges of the fold with gimp pins (not ordinary fine tacks). The use of gimp pins overcomes the possibility of studs hitting the heads of tacks.

Note This seat does not require a lining and no raw edges are visible on the underside of the chair.

Circular Stool with Welted Cover (traditional method and materials)

Some stools, particularly piano stools, have seats which can be raised or lowered by means of a central screw. Such stools are highly sought after, and are becoming increasingly hard to find. They should be re-upholstered using traditional materials and methods. Unlike the articles previously described, the base of these stools is a solid piece of wood, and will therefore not need webbing.

Upholstering the stool

1. Cut an accurate pattern of the top of the wooden base. As you will need this for various stages of the work, cut it from strong paper. Fold the pattern into four and mark points N, S, E and W on the edge of the paper.
2. Place the pattern on the stool and mark the quarter points on the wood with chalk.
3. Attach the bridles to the base. As there is no hessian on the wood, you cannot stitch the twine to the base, so insert a series of 10-mm ($\frac{3}{8}$-in) fine tacks around the stool 4 cm (1$\frac{1}{2}$ in) in from the edge and approximately 8 cm (3 in) apart. Hammer the tacks lightly into the wood to about a third of their length. Then take a length of stitching twine, twist one end of this around one tack and drive the tack home. Place your left hand on the

board close to this tack, take the twine over your hand and twist it round the second tack to secure. Continue fixing the other bridles in the same way until you have a complete circle (figure 24).
4. Take coir or hair stuffing and work it under the bridles, building up the stuffing to a depth of 5-7 cm (2-3 in) depending on the desired height of the finished stool. You may find it necessary to make the bridles looser for a very deep seat. Tease the fibre and ensure that you obtain a firm and level surface.
5. Place the paper pattern of the seat on a length of scrim and draw around it. This marks the stitching line. Mark a cutting line 1·5 cm ($\frac{3}{4}$ in) outside this line and cut out the circle. Mark N, S, E and W with a pen. Cut the welt or box 12 cm (5 in) deep and to a length equal to the circumference of the pattern plus 5 cm (2 in) for turnings at the ends.
6. Machine on a line 2 cm ($\frac{3}{4}$ in) from one long edge of the welt using a very fine stitch. Slash the 2-cm ($\frac{3}{4}$-in) allowance on the welt (figure 25). With the box section towards the front, fit this around the circle of scrim. The slashed edge will open out to give a clean seam free from any fullness in the box. Join the ends of the box section and stitch the seam making sure the stitching runs down the thread of the scrim. When fitting the box to the circle, insert the pins on the line of machine stitching on the box and bring them out on the marked line on the circle.
7. Place the cover over the stuffing and draw it down to the top edge of the wooden base. If the edge of the base is bevelled, tack the scrim to this edge; if not, tack it to the top of the side edge. Turn up the excess scrim and tack at intervals. Trim to 1 cm ($\frac{1}{2}$ in).
8. Work a row of blind-stitching and two rows of top-stitching round the stool (figures 14-19). Use a regulator for a uniformly

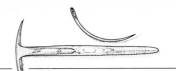

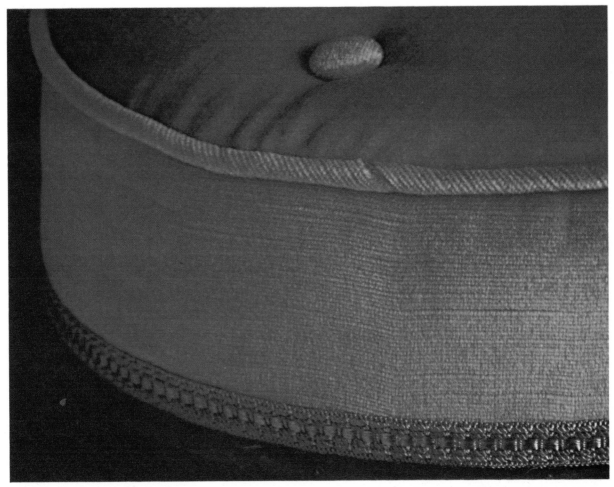

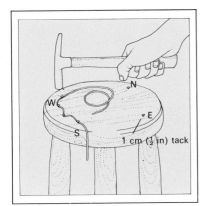

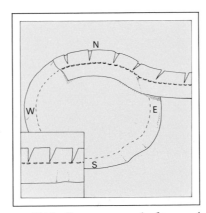

(Left) Circular stool upholstered with the traditional methods and materials; the stuffing was stitched with blind and top stitching, and the cover boxed, piped and buttoned

(Above) Detail of piano stool on left showing the boxed edge, the style of joining the piping ends, the top buttoning, and neatening effect of the edging braid

firm edge. Check that the rows of stitching and the tacks follow the lines of the threads of the scrim.

9. Work a second circle of bridles 4 cm (1½ in) in from the edge of the upholstery and insert a thin layer of stuffing. Make sure the stuffing is slightly thicker in the centre of the stool to give a domed shape.

10. Using the paper pattern, cut a circle of wadding. Place over the top stuffing.

11. Make an undercover of calico in the same way as the scrim cover, and place this over the seat. Tack to the side of the seat placing the tacks just below those in stage 7. Keep the depth of the box uniform all round the stool. Trim away the surplus calico. Make sure that you keep the sides absolutely straight up and down for a neat appearance.

24 Fix circle of bridles on top of stool anchoring twine with fine tacks

25 Slash allowance on welt, fit around circle of scrim

Making up the outer cover

12. Using the paper pattern, cut the top circle from your chosen fabric. (Using this pattern throughout will ensure that the sides of the stool remain vertical and that no fullness appears around the lower edge of the box.) Pipe the top circle of the cover exactly on the stitching line, using piping cord covered with strips of fabric cut on the true cross. Fit this piping on a flat surface rather than over your fingers which may make the edge fluted. Tack the box in place. Stitch the seam using a zipper or piping foot, then trim the covering of the piping cord to 3 mm ($\frac{1}{8}$ in)—this prevents four layers of cover fabric appearing as a ridge on the right side of the finished work.

13. Place the cover in position and arrange the seam allowance so that it faces downwards under the box section of the cover. Tack along the lower edge of the wooden base and trim away any surplus box fabric.

14. Using a scroll gimp, neaten the lower edge of the cover. Place the gimp around the stool with the wrong side outside. Stretch it slightly and pin the two ends together. Remove it from the stool taking care the pin does not fall out. Back-stitch along the seam and spread a little adhesive where the surplus gimp is to be cut away. Let this dry and then trim the surplus. Replace it on the stool and secure with matching gimp pins.

Note A lining is not necessary on this style of stool.

Traditional upholstery methods and materials meet modern upholstery methods and materials: the bedroom chair was traditionally upholstered with coir fibre and wadding, calico and canvas; the dressing stool and footstool were upholstered with the modern materials of various foams which are dealt with in detail in the following pages. They show that traditional and modern can mix

Re-upholstering a Drop-in Seat (modern method and materials)

1. Strip the frame and check its size in the same way as for upholstering a drop-in seat by the traditional method.

2. To web the base, mark the centre points of the back and front rails of the frame. Arrange the webs so that the distance between them is not greater than the width of the webbing itself. Attaching the centre web first, place the edge, point A, of the webbing 1 cm ($\frac{1}{2}$ in) in from the back edge of the frame, and secure with three 15-mm ($\frac{5}{8}$-in) improved tacks.

3. Bring the webbing to the front of the frame and mark with a felt pen where it crosses the front edge. Measure the length of the webbing (figure 26). Calculate one-tenth of this distance and mark back from B for point C. Stretch the webbing so that point C reaches the edge of the frame and secure with three improved tacks (figure 27). Cut off the webbing 5 mm ($\frac{1}{4}$ in) back from the edge of the frame.

Note Hammer in the tacks so that their tops are quite flat, otherwise the tops will cut into the webbing.

4. Attach the other vertical webs, then weave in the horizontals, stretching each by one-tenth of its length. (It is the stretch which makes these seats comfortable.) On larger seats, stretch the webbing by one-eighth of the length rather than one-tenth.

Note Do not place hessian over this rubberized webbing or its advantages will be lost.

Choosing and cutting the foam

Use 25-mm (1-in) solid foam of medium-firm density.

5. Make a paper pattern of the frame and place this on the foam. Using a felt pen, mark round the pattern. Draw a second line 1 cm ($\frac{1}{2}$ in)

outside this first marking and cut along it using kitchen scissors. The foam, this will be half way up the edge of the foam.

6. The edges should be 'feathered' (figure 28) to give a smooth, rounded edge to the upholstery. To do this, cut back the edges of the foam at an angle of 45° to within 1 cm (½ in) of the top of the foam. In the case of 25-mm (1-in) solid foam, feather to half way up the edge of the foam (diagram 19).

Covering the foam with calico

7. Tear 0·3-m (9-in) fine unbleached calico into three equal strips, each 10 cm (3 in) wide.

Note One strip is usually enough for the two side pieces. Iron these strips so that the torn edges are quite flat. Cut each strip so that it is the length of the foam plus 8 cm (3 in) at each end to overhang (figure 29).

8. Using a felt pen, mark a border 4 cm (1½ in) wide all round the top unfeathered surface of the foam. In addition, mark a line on the calico strips parallel to the torn edges and 4 cm (1½ in) in from the edge.

9. Spread the border around the foam and the narrower of the two 4-cm (1½-in) borders of the calico strip with a thin layer of upholstery adhesive. It is most important that both these surfaces are completely covered. Leave them to dry—i.e. until the adhesive, which is shiny and sticky when applied, becomes dull-looking.

10. Take the strip of calico to be fitted to the front of the foam and lower it into position. Make sure there is an equal overhang at each end and that the torn edge of the calico reaches up to, but does not cover, the marked border on the foam. Smooth down the fluffy torn edges so that they merge into the foam and do not leave a hard line that could show through the top

11. Attach the strip to the back of the foam, then the side strips.

12. Mark the mid-points of the front and back of the foam and place it on a table, calico surface down. Place the frame centrally on the foam with the webbed side downwards so that the webbing touches the foam. There should now be a border of foam, 1 cm (½ in) wide, visible all round the frame, and the

(Right) Modern carver dining chair with drop-in seat on which solid foam has been used over Pirelli webbing

(Below) Underside of drop-in seat on which the Pirelli webbing has been used, combined with traditional stuffing and consequently with hessian

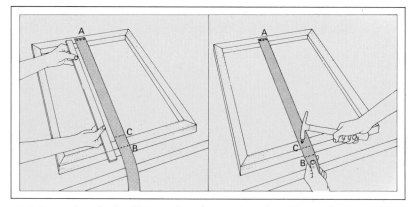

26 *Measure length of webbing and mark B at front edge*

27 *Stretch webbing to bring point C to front edge*

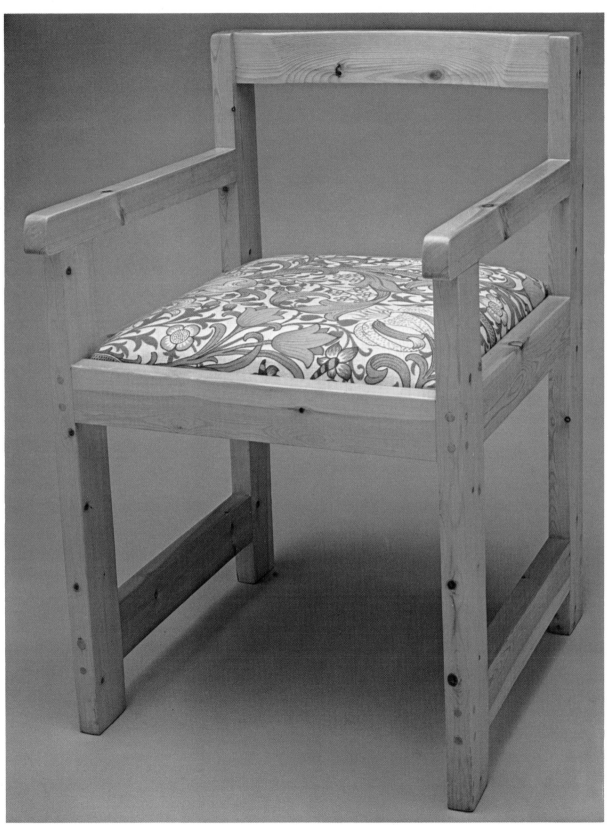

mid-points of the foam and frame should be in a line.

13. With the back edge of the frame away from you, take the free edge of the calico along this edge and, tucking in the 1 cm ($\frac{1}{2}$ in) of foam, bring the calico up on to the top of the frame, i.e. the underside of the finished seat. Secure in the centre of the rail with a 10-mm ($\frac{3}{8}$-in) fine tack. Turn the frame round and repeat on the front edge.

(Far left) Occasional chair with drop-in seat on which 50-mm (2-in) foam has been used; the back has been upholstered as for a pin-cushion seat with 25-mm (1-in) foam
(Left) Detail of drop-in seat shown opposite: the lining has been tacked to the underside of the frame to neaten all cut edges

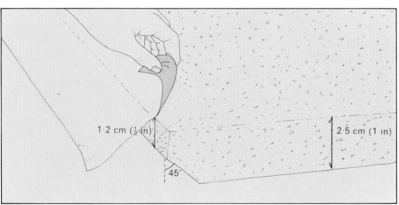

28 *Edges of foam feathered at 45° and calico strip attached*

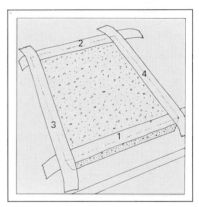

29 *Allow strips to overhang at each end*

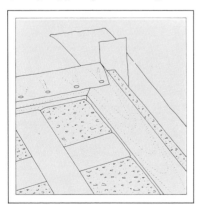

30 *Slash front and back strips along the edge of frame*

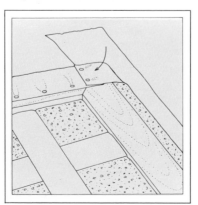

31 *Bring end of front and back strip to underside of frame and tack*

32 *Corner of side strips overhang front and back strips*

35

14. Returning to the back edge, begin the permanent tacking. Take out the temporary tack, re-tighten the calico and secure. Work outwards from this central tack to the ends of the back rail. Check that the edge of the foam comes right up to the edge of the top of the frame, but that no foam comes down over the edge of the frame. If this happens, the completed seat will not fit back into the chair. The 1-cm ($\frac{1}{2}$-in) border of foam allows the foam to curve round, giving a well-padded edge. This also prevents the foam splitting (figure 31). Tack the front strip of calico in a similar way. Insert the tacks approximately 1 cm ($\frac{1}{2}$ in) in from the edge of the frame and 2 cm ($\frac{3}{4}$ in) apart.

15. There will be a length of unused calico at each end of the front and back strips. To finish the end of one of these, slash the strip along the edge of the frame to the corner and then open it out. Turn the frame sideways, tuck in 1 cm ($\frac{1}{2}$ in) of foam and bring up the end of the strip to the top of the frame. Trim away any surplus. Repeat at the other three corners.

Note You have not yet touched the side strips.

16. Complete tacking the side strips as along the front and back, working as far as the corners.

17. To finish the corners, slash the side strips along the edge of the wood (figure 31) and open out the strip. This strip will be free where it has passed over the first strip. Bring it over the top of the first strip so that it lies flat and mark with a pen the line it reaches on the under layer of calico. Spread this with adhesive. Allow to dry and secure the top strip of calico in position. It will be at an angle of approximately 45° to the edge of the frame (figure 32). Take it to the underside of the frame and secure with two tacks.

When the tacking is complete, you will see that the foam tends to balloon away from the webbing. Do not worry about this. If you attach the cover properly, it will compress the foam, bringing it down on to the webbing and making for greater comfort.

Attaching the outer cover

18. It is not usually necessary to use wadding or add an undercover when using solid foam. However, if the top fabric has a shiny surface, it might be wise to add a very thin undercover. This will reduce the strain on the top cover and so avoid 'tack-draws'. These are shadowy lines which run from a tack into the centre of the seat and they are usually caused by over-tightening, using too few tacks or using a fabric which is too loosely woven or has a highly glossy finish.

When attaching the top cover, stroke it very firmly to the front edge after tacking the back edge; it is the pressure applied that brings the foam down on to the webbing and gives the final seat a good shape. The foam is compressed during this process and gives added resilience to the seat. It is essential that the tightening of the cover is done by stroking with the *flat* of your hand over a wide area, rather than pulling in a very restricted area with a thumb and finger. The latter results in a wavy edge to the work, particularly when foam is being used.

Tack the sides and finish off the corners as described for the seat upholstered by traditional methods (stages 15–18).

Lining the seat

Choose a lining that is very closely woven to exclude the light from the foam. Cut out, prepare and attach in the same way as for a drop-in seat upholstered by the traditional method.

Circular Footstool (modern method and materials)

The upholstery technique described here may be applied to a new or an old stool which has a central piece of wood that fits into a recessed groove on a solid base. It is anchored by a metal or wooden screw. If the base is very old, strip it with great care. Do not strip across the base as the wood on such stools is often soft and prone to split.

Upholstering the stool

1. Cut polyurethane foam 5 cm (2 in) larger than the base (this allows for a 2·5-cm/1-in border round the base). This type of foam is perfectly satisfactory for upholstering this type of stool as the seat will not be subjected to heavy wear or pressure.

2. From a piece of fine calico 0·5 m ($\frac{1}{2}$ yd) long, prepare four strips, each 8 cm (3 in) wide. Tear them parallel to the short edges of the fabric so that each strip is 0·5 m

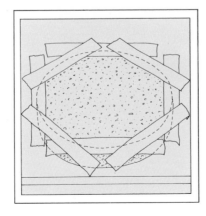

33 *Attach strips*

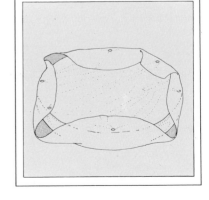

34 *Insert tacks at opposite points*

(Above) Footstool with drop-in centre
(Left) 50-mm (2-in) foam used

($\frac{1}{2}$ yd) long. Divide each strip into two, making sure the strips are long enough to form an overhang, when in position, of approximately 1 cm ($\frac{1}{2}$ in) at each end (figure 33). Iron all the strips.

3. Using a felt pen, mark the lines as shown in figure 33 and spread the area between these lines and the edge of the foam with a thin layer of adhesive.

4. Draw a line the width of A-B from one torn edge of each strip, spread with adhesive and allow to dry.

5. Attach the strips in the order shown in figure 33, taking care not to cover the marked lines. Do not apply adhesive where the diagonal strips overlap the first four strips. These should remain free at this stage.

6. Place the foam, calicoed surface downwards, on a table, and position the wooden circle centrally on top of it. Tuck in the 2·5-cm (1-in) border of foam at the centre of the

first strip, then bring up the calico to the top of the base and secure using a 10-mm ($\frac{3}{8}$-in) tack. Turn the base through 180° and repeat with strips two, three and four.

7. Return to the first strip and, working outwards from the central tack, complete the tacking of this strip. Keep the tacks close to the edge of the wood to avoid bulk.

Note Bring the calico down tightly to the base of the wood. Because the edge is curved, the width of calico being drawn over the edge will increase until the whole width is on top of the base.

Repeat the procedure with strips 2, 3 and 4. Trim away all surplus fabric.

8. Take the centre of the fifth strip, bring it up on to the base and tack. Tighten and tack for approximately 2·5 cm (1 in) either side of this central tack. You will find that, at these points, the inner edge of the strip is now no longer anchored. Allow one end to lie flat on the foam, mark where it falls on the seat and secure with adhesive. Secure the other end in the same way and complete tacking along the strip.

Repeat with the other three strips and trim accordingly.

9. Place the wadding over the foam and trim so that the edge is 1 cm (½ in) above the edge of the foam. Tease away the underside of the wadding to prevent a ridge showing through the cover.

10. Place the undercover, i.e. the remaining piece of the calico, over the wadding.

Draw the calico to the underside of the base and anchor at its most northern point. Smooth with the flat of the hand over the foam to the opposite (southern) point and tack. Then secure from the eastern to the western points on the seat.

Note This is different from the treatment for a 'rectangular' seat.

11. Stroking outwards from the centre of the seat (figure 34), insert diagonal tacks, i.e. from north-west to south-east. Continue in this way, dividing the space between the tacks until they are 2 cm (¾ in) apart. Keep them as close to the edge of the wood as possible. Insert each row just inside the previous row. Trim away all surplus calico.

12. Iron the outer cover and attach in the same way. Trim this very neatly (it is not usual to line the underside of such a base, because such lining would produce extra bulk and tend to lift the upholstered section above the rebate of the surrounding wood).

Pin-cushion Seat (modern method and materials)

1. Strip the chair with care and make a paper pattern of the upholstered area.

2. Place the pattern on a piece of very closely woven hessian, so that the back edge of the pattern runs along the grain of the material. Draw around the pattern and then draw a second line 2 cm (¾ in) outside the pattern. Cut along this outer line.

3. Turn in the edge of the hessian, slightly in excess of the 2 cm (¾ in) allowed. Place the back folded edge just inside the rebate along the back of the chair and secure with gimp pins (these will damage the frame less than tacks). Complete tacking the hessian in position but do not over-tighten.

4. Web the seat with 5-cm (2-in) Pirelli webbing, as for the drop-in seat (figure 26) but use five 10-mm (⅜-in) improved tacks to attach the webbing to the frame.

5. Use 22-mm (1-in) solid latex foam for the seat. Reduce the paper pattern by 3 mm (⅛ in) all round and place this on the foam. Mark the outline with a felt pen and cut along this line.

To obtain a gently sloping edge, feather the foam to a point all round its edges by cutting at an angle of about 30° (figure 35).

6. Tear two strips of calico for each edge of the foam, allowing an overhang of 1 cm (½ in) at each end.

7. Using a felt pen, draw a border

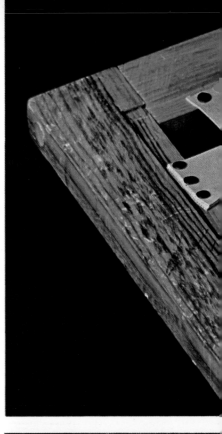

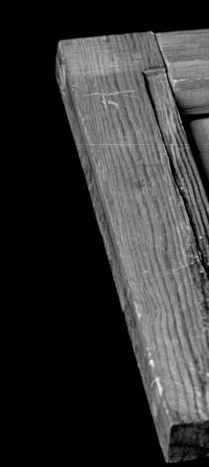

(Top) Cross section of a pin-cushion seat showing 25-mm (1-in) solid foam on Pirelli webbing tacked to the narrow rebate: note feathering used to obtain domed effect

(Bottom) Method of re-upholstering used when the top surface of the rebate has been badly damaged; the Pirelli webbing has been tacked to the underside of the seat and in addition to the feathered solid foam a layer of polyurethane foam has been inserted

4 cm (1½ in) wide round the foam on both the feathered and the top surfaces. Spread these borders with a thin layer of adhesive.

8. Draw a line 4 cm (1½ in) in from one torn edge of each strip and spread with adhesive.

9. Place the front and back strips of calico on the top, i.e. the un-feathered surface of the foam. Then attach the side strips. Turn the foam over and attach the other four strips to the feathered edge.

10. Insert a 10-mm (⅜-in) tack through the calico, right up to the foam at each corner of the rebated border of wood. Position one tack at each corner of the rebated border of wood (figure 36).

11. Tack along the back edge, plac-ing the tacks to follow the line of the chair and piercing the calico on the line of the foam. Do not drive the tacks home until the foam is secured on all four sides. Check that the tacks are in a smooth line running parallel to the outline of the polished wood. When correctly positioned, drive them home. Trim away all surplus calico.

12. Place the outer cover over the foam—no wadding or undercover are necessary. Tack along the inside of the back rebate, keeping the tacks as close to the edge of this rebate as possible. Stroke the cover firmly towards the front edge with the flat of your hand and tack along the front edge. Complete as for the traditionally upholstered seat.

Kitchen Stool Upholstered with Foam (modern method and materials)

As this involves the making of a completely new item, rather than upholstering an existing one, a list of materials required is provided for convenience. The materials are:

3-4 plastic-coated legs

a circular base of 20-mm (¾-in) blockboard, 36-40 (14-15 in) in diameter

a circle of foam, 50 or 75 mm (2 or 3 in) deep and 6 mm (¼ in) larger in diameter than the base

0·5 m (½ yd) calico, 120 cm (48 in) wide

0·5 m (½ yd) vinyl for the cover

2 m (2½ yd) nylon piping cord, 3 mm (⅛ in) in diameter

tacks and adhesive

When using any kind of foam on a solid base, you must bore ventila-tion holes of 1 cm (½ in) diameter in the wood (figure 38). This will allow the air contained in the foam to escape silently when the stool is in use. If you are intending to use a vinyl-type fabric, rather than one of woven material, these ventilation holes are even more important.

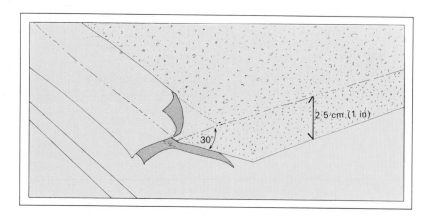

35 Feather foam at angle of 30°, double calico strips protect thin foam

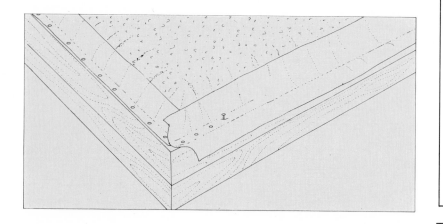

36 Tack calico to rebated border, tacks being 5 mm (¼ in) from outer edge of rebate

> **Hints**
>
> Stool legs are usually sold in sets of four, but some people prefer to use only three for a kitchen stool.
>
> Make sure that the ventilation holes are large enough for the air to escape.
>
> Always work from an accurate pattern. Always cut the cover on the article being upholstered.
>
> Take care that the sides of your foam-padded seats are vertical.
>
> Apply adhesive to both surfaces and allow to dry before joining them together.

Kitchen stool re-covered with vinyl

(Above) Detail showing method of tacking lining to corners of stools. The lining is slashed at the leg

(Right) Kidney-shaped dress stool made as a kitchen stool: the base has a removable skirted cover

Upholstering the stool

1. Decide on the position of the legs, trace their outline on the base but do not attach them or the bases into which they are screwed at this stage. Mark and bore the ventilation holes.

2. Make a paper pattern of the top of the stool and place this on the foam. Mark the outline with a felt-tipped pen. Draw a second line 3 mm ($\frac{1}{8}$ in) outside the first line. Cut along this second line keeping the edge smooth and *absolutely* vertical.

3. Spread a 2·5-cm (1-in) border of adhesive around the outside of the upper surface of the wooden base. Spread a similar band on one surface of the foam and allow both to dry.

4. Place the foam on the base, compressing it so that the two outside edges of the foam and wood fit exactly. This will ensure that the edge of the stool is well padded and prevent sharp edges developing.

5. Tear a strip of calico 6 cm (2 in) wide and long enough to go right around the stool.

Note It may be necessary to use two pieces, in which case, do not join them but apply them to the foam so that they meet edge to edge. Iron the strips.

6. Spread a layer of adhesive around the bottom 2-cm (1-in) edge of the foam, i.e. just above its junction with the base. Spread a similar band of adhesive over half the width of the calico. Allow the adhesive to dry and place the calico around the foam, the free edge of the calico will come down over the edge of the wooden base (figure 37).

7. Place the stool with the foam on a table and, holding the free edge of the calico firmly, tack this to the top edge of the base; you will find that the tacks penetrate the block-

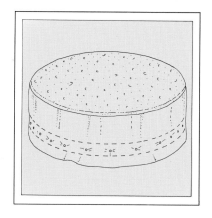

37 Attach calico to overhang base without compressing foam

board very easily. If using plywood, you will find that the tacks tend to cause the laminated layers to separate.

8. Make up the cover, as for the piano stool. No calico undercover is necessary with this type of cover. The top of the foam will appear larger than the base of the stool, but use the cover to bring it back to the correct size otherwise fullness will appear at the lower edge of the box. Use the pattern made for the foam to cut the circle for the cover, allowing 1-cm ($\frac{1}{2}$-in) turnings.

Note When using vinyl to cover piping cord, there is no need to cut it on the cross (not being woven, this material has no cross). Avoid coarse piping cords which produce a bulky edging.

9. Place the cover in position. It will appear too small at this stage, but do not worry. Using the blade of a round-ended knife, press the top edge of the foam back to the seam of the cover and insert a temporary tack anchoring the cover to the underside of the base. Repeat this process at the opposite side of the stool and then at quarterly intervals. Complete the tacking, using the knife to obtain a smooth edge. When tacking to the underside of the base, keep the tacks as close to the edge of the frame as is possible without splintering the wood. This is to avoid bulk. If the cover is made of a very thick material, do not take it to the underside of the stool but tack it to the bottom of the edge of the base and neaten with matching banding and enamelled studs. Cover the studs with a cloth when driving them in to avoid damage.

10. Line the underside of the seat and attach the sockets for the legs. Screw the legs into the sockets to complete the stool.

> *There are special upholstery adhesives available. Use one made for latex and synthetic foams —clear, yet pliable when dry.*

Rectangular Dressing Stool Upholstered with Foam (modern method and materials)

Again, this is a completely new item of furniture. You will need:
20-mm ($\frac{3}{4}$-in) thick blockboard, measuring 35 × 45 cm (13 × 18 in)
1 set traditional Queen Anne-style legs
50-mm (2-in) thick foam, measuring 35·5 × 45·5 cm (13$\frac{1}{4}$ × 18$\frac{1}{4}$ in)
12-mm ($\frac{1}{2}$-in) thick foam, measuring 25 × 35 cm (9 × 14 in)
0·7 m ($\frac{3}{4}$ yd) calico
0·5 m ($\frac{1}{2}$ yd) wadding
tacks and adhesive

Preparing the base

1. Attach the legs to the base of the stool with wood glue, reinforcing each one with three screws. Insert these from the upper surface of the base, through the blockboard into the legs. Alternatively you may find there are ready-drilled holes in the legs through which you can countersink the screws into the base.

2. Bore the ventilation holes (figure 38).

Attaching the foam to the base

3. Check that the sides of the 5-cm (2-in) thick foam are absolutely vertical so that the finished stool will have well-shaped edges.

4. Feather the 12-mm ($\frac{1}{2}$-in)-thick foam to a point as before and position it centrally on the upperside of the base. This will act as a 'doming' and give the stool a good shape (figure 39). Check that the

Dressing stool with seat worked with a square edge as with the kitchen stool; 50-mm (2-in) pin core foam has been used over 25-mm (1-in) doming: the sides have been finished with piped edging and scroll gimp

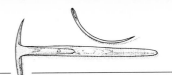

border around the doming is an even 5 cm (2 in) all round, otherwise the stool will appear one-sided.

5. Spread a layer of adhesive around the outer 2 cm (1 in) of the upper surface of the stool. Spread a similar border of adhesive on one surface of the large rectangle of foam.

Position the four corners of the foam to the four corners of the base of the stool with great care. Compress the foam so that the edges of the sides of the foam fit the sides of the base perfectly.

6. Tear two strips of calico to measure 45 x 5 cm (18 x 2 in) and two strips 35 x 5 cm (13 x 2 in). Draw a line down the centre of the strips and spread a layer of adhesive to cover half of each one. Spread a layer of adhesive 2·5 cm (1 in) wide around the lower half of each side of the foam. When the adhesive is dry, apply one strip of calico to each side of the foam, the free edge of the strips falling over the base of the stool as on the kitchen stool.

(Right) Detail of upholstered–over stool with polished wood surround: the cover has two balanced pleats at the corner and the edge has been neatened by attaching textured braid which can be used as an alternative to scroll gimp

(Below) Another view of the drop-in stool showing worked canvas cover

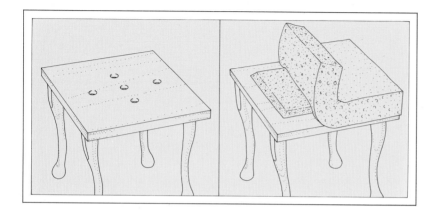

38 *Bore ventilation holes*   39 *Doming effect*

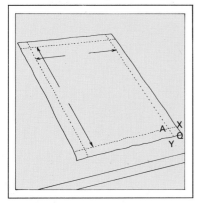

40 *Mark out calico*

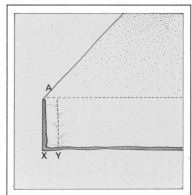

41 *Fold calico*

42 *Stitch and trim*

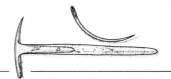

Stool with worked canvas cover that has been treated as an upholstered-over seat: the cover has two balanced pleats at each corner and the edges have been neatened with a worked canvas braid

7. Tack the free calico to the edge of the blockboard, keeping it taut. Trim off the calico below the level of the tacks. The foam will have spread outwards around its top edge, so bring it back to the size of the base by attaching a well-fitting undercover.

8. Mark the calico as in figure 40. At the first corner, fold the fabric along the line marked A-Q so that A-X lies over A-Y (figure 41). Tack and stitch along A-X and trim to 3 mm ($\frac{1}{8}$ in) (figure 42). This results in a square corner. Repeat with the other three corners.

9. Place the cover over the foam and insert a tack on each side of the four corners. Use a knife to press back the top edge of the foam and tack the sides of the undercover to the top of the sides of the block-board. Check that the depth of the box is uniform all round, and that the edge of the seat is crisp and square. The top of the seat should now measure 45 x 35 cm (18 x 13 in) to correspond with the wooden base.

10. Cut a rectangle of wadding to the size of the wooden base and place it on the top of the calico undercover, skin side uppermost. Slip-stitch the wadding to the calico.

11. Cut the outer cover. You can make this up in two ways. If you are using a thick or pile fabric (e.g. fur fabric) make it up in the same way as the calico undercover (figures 40, 41, 42). Alternatively, if incorporating a piped edging, cut as shown in figure 43.

Join the box sections leaving the top 1 cm ($\frac{1}{2}$ in) unstitched. Pipe around the top rectangle, pinning the piping to the stitching line and slashing at the corners for a smooth fit. Fit the corners of the box to the corners of the top of the cover and then fit the intervening sections.

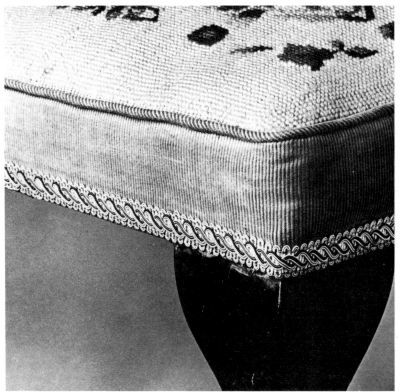

(Top left) Detail showing the finish of an underside cut away corner
(Bottom left) Detail of boxed edge showing use of piping and scroll gimp
(Right) Upholstered-over stool showing use of pattern on fabric

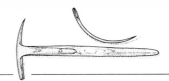

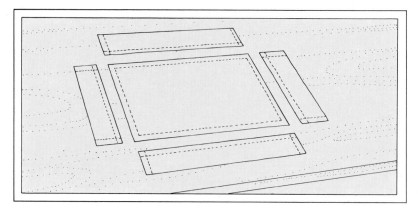

43 *Method of cutting material for tailored cover*

Tack and stitch with a piping foot. Trim away the seam allowances of the piping to stagger the layers. Fit the cover over the wadding and draw the box down to the lower edge of the base. Check that the seam allowance is facing downwards under the box and insert a tack 6 mm ($\frac{1}{4}$ in) on each side of the four corners.

Complete the tacking of the four sides of the cover, keeping the tacks along the bottom edge of the base. Trim off surplus fabric and neaten the raw edge with a scroll gimp attached with gimp pins. Make a template on the underside of the base and cut a lining to fit. Tack in position.

12. Rub the wooden legs with fine glass paper working with the grain of the wood. Stain and finish with a wax polish or polyurethane.

Upholstered and Buttoned Headboard (modern method and materials)

Spongeable materials and modern equipment have made the job of cleaning upholstery a much easier task than it was in the past. As a result, this type of headboard has regained its popularity. The various attachments of a vacuum cleaner can be used to remove surface dust, or the headboard can be sprayed with an aerosol cleaner. Vinyl-type materials need no more than a gentle wipe with a soapy cloth.

Choose the covering fabric to match the curtains in the room or choose a plain fabric to highlight one of the colours in a patterned carpet.

When choosing the cover fabric, care must be taken with regard to the width. For a single bedhead, choose fabric 120 cm (48 in) wide, and use it so that the warp threads (i.e. those running parallel to the selvedges) run from the top to the bottom of the bedhead. For double and king-size bedheads, you may find it necessary to join several widths of fabric together or, preferably, use the fabric with the warp threads running from side to side of the board.

The covering of a headboard is one of the few occasions when it is correct to use velvet with the pile running across the work. Dralon velvet is a very practical and popular material for buttoned headboards.

If the fabric you have chosen has a floral design, it may be necessary to join part-widths of fabric each side of a central panel, in order to ensure that the flowers are 'growing' vertically.

Choosing the headboard

This can be the most expensive item of the project. An old wooden headboard is ideal to use as a base for an upholstered board, but you will not be able to restore it to its original form for re-use because of the holes bored through it.

If using a new base, one made of 12·5-mm ($\frac{1}{2}$-in) chipboard or block-board is the most suitable.

It is important to choose a base which will not warp. Keep the shape simple with an outline that is smooth and flowing and avoid any shape which has deep indentations and sharp points.

Choosing the buttons

For deep buttoning, the button moulds are usually covered with the fabric used for the bedhead itself. If the covering fabric is not too thick, buy moulds from a haberdashery department and cover them yourself. If you are using a thick or pile fabric, you may find it easier to have the button moulds covered professionally. An upholsterer may do this for you; otherwise, you can send the fabric to a button-covering service. Buttons measuring 1-2 cm ($\frac{1}{2}$-$\frac{3}{4}$ in) in diameter give the best results.

Choosing the foam

Polyurethane foam can be used very satisfactorily on bedheads, and it would really be a waste of money to use latex foam in this case. For deep buttoning, 70-75mm (2-3 in) foam is recommended, but for shallow-buttoning 25-mm (1-in) foam is quite adequate. Before cutting it, decide whether you wish to upholster the whole board or to leave the lower portion non-upholstered so that it fits behind the mattress. When creating a completely new board, leave this non-

Attaching the undercover and starting to prepare the button recesses on an upholstered, buttoned headboard: it is best to work diagonally and to pin the pleats between buttons .

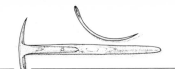

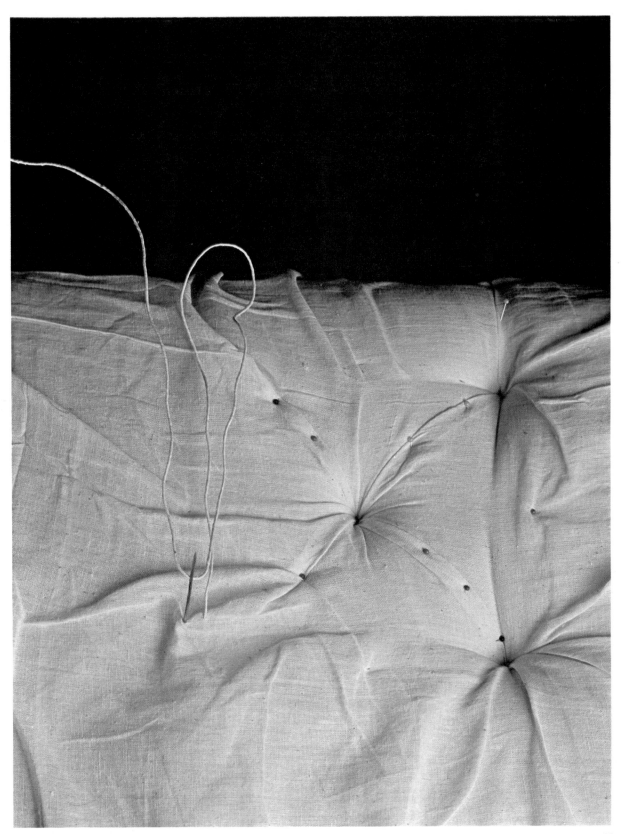

upholstered border to a depth of 10-15 cm (4-6 in) so that it fits closely to the mattress. This prevents the pillows disappearing between the mattress and the bedhead.

Make a paper pattern of the section of the board to be upholstered. Place the pattern on the foam, leaving a border of 2·5 cm (1 in) round the pattern. Draw round the cutting outline and then cut the foam with kitchen scissors or a sharp carving knife. Keep the edge of the foam vertical to give a uniform and well-padded outline to the finished work.

Estimating the quantity of fabric

Be very careful about this: it is easy to ruin a piece of work by allowing too little fabric initially. Count the number of buttons on the longest row (7 buttons on figure 44). Calculate the amount of fabric required as follows:
1 width of board plus 2 x depth of foam plus 2 x depth of wood plus 7 x half depth of foam plus 5 cm (2 in).
These last two measurements allow

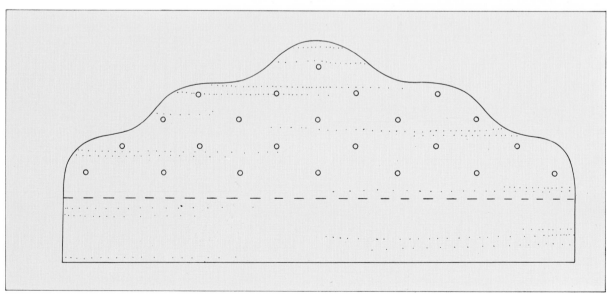

44 *Buttoned headboard showing possible positions of buttons, no button less than 7 cm (3 in) from edge*

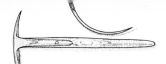

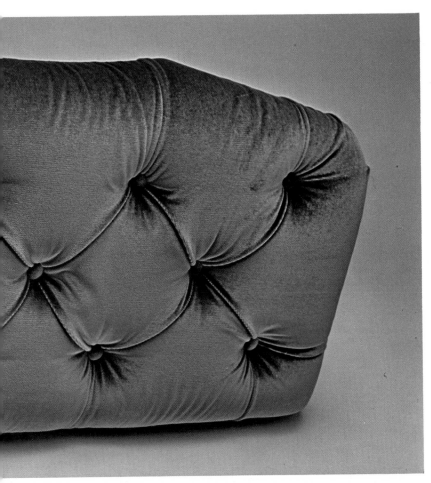

for the depth of the buttoning and for the fabric to be taken to the back of the board. Calculate the amount of fabric required for a double-sized bedhead, with seven buttons on the long rows and using 75-mm (3-in) foam, as follows:

138 cm plus 15 cm plus 2·5 cm plus 26·5 cm plus 5 cm = a total of 187 cm. (54 in plus 6 in plus 1 in plus 10½ in plus 2 in = 73½ in.)
So buy 1·9 m (2⅛ yd) fabric 120 cm (48 in) wide, together with an equal amount of thin calico.

Planning the buttoning

Mark off the bottom area of the board which is not to be upholstered. The diamond is the most popular pattern for buttoning and you can vary the size and shape to suit the shape of your board, the number of buttons you are using and the texture of the covering fabric. Mark the horizontal rows

Upholstered, buttoned headboard for a single bed, without a rebate below the upholstery for the mattress: on this board 75-mm (3-in) foam was used, the outer cover is in Dralon velvet

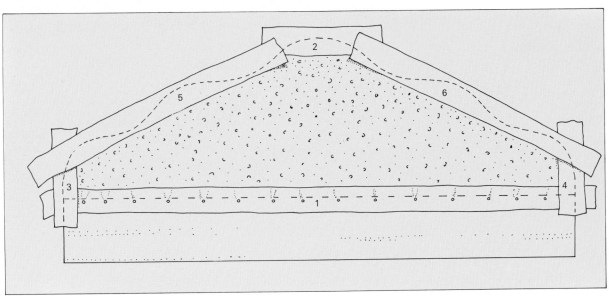

45 *Attach strips and tack lower edge, non-upholstered section fits behind mattress*

from 10-15 cm (4-6 in) apart and the buttons from 20-25 cm (8-10 in). Note however that no button should be less than 8 cm (3 in) from the edge of the board or you will lose the smooth outline. Mark the positions of the buttons and check these very carefully. Bore a 4-mm ($\frac{1}{8}$-in) hole at each mark. Test to see if a threaded mattress needle will pass through one of the holes easily.

Preparing the foam

1. Tear three strips of calico each 10 cm (4 in) wide and parallel to the selvedge of the material. If you tear them from the end of the length, the remaining piece of calico will not be the right size to use as the undercover. Iron the strips, then cut them into suitable lengths (figure 45).
2. Spread a border of adhesive around the foam and over a 5-cm (2-in)-wide band down each strip. Attach the top and bottom strips to the foam, then the side strips and finally any diagonal pieces.

Attaching the foam to the board

3. Place the underside of the board on a table. Insert five 10-mm ($\frac{3}{8}$-in) fine tacks along the lower edge of the foam to pass through the calico at the extreme edge of the foam (figure 45). Drive these lightly into the wood along the lower edge of the part to be upholstered. Then, holding the foam firmly to the board, turn the whole piece of work over so that the foam is on the table and the back of the board uppermost.
4. Bring the free calico from the top strip to the back of the board, tucking in the extra foam. Tack the calico to the wood. Insert the tacks

Detail of the buttoning of an upholstered bedhead: the pleating should be so arranged that it faces downwards in order to avoid collecting dust

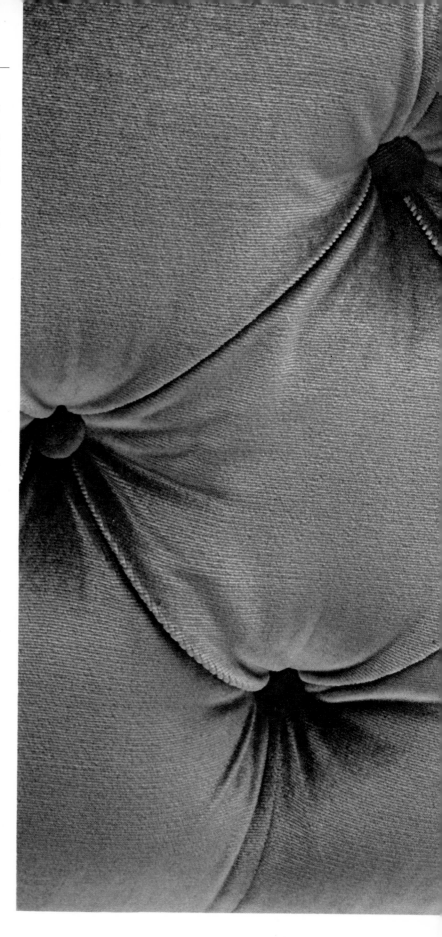

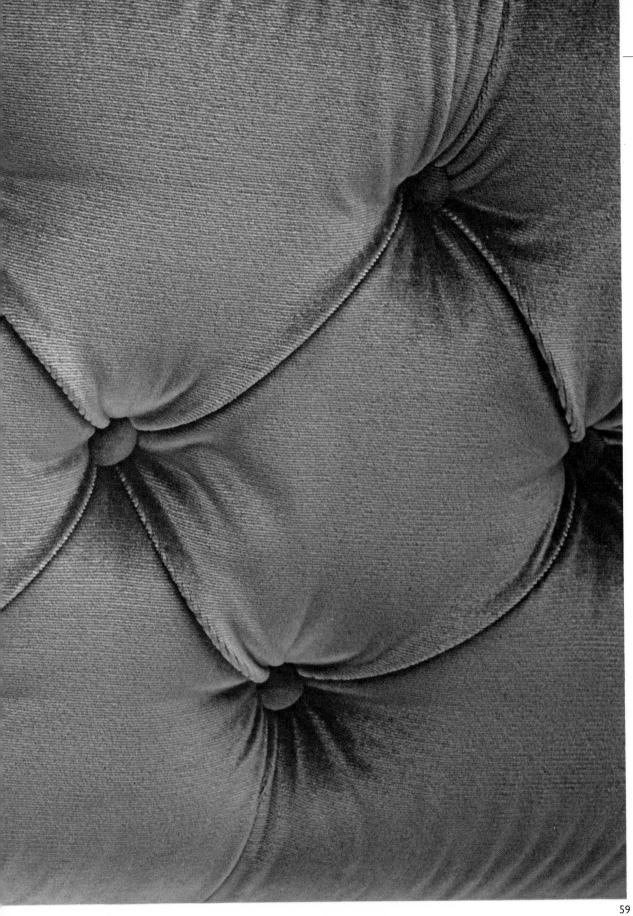

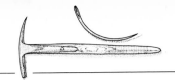

Buttoned-backed sewing chair: the seat was built up as for a kitchen stool, using 125-mm (5-in) foam: the back was buttoned, using 50-mm (2-in) foam

1 cm (½ in) in from the edge and about the same distance apart. Anchor the side strips next and finally attach the diagonal strips. Turn the headboard over and complete the tacking of the lower edge. Keep the tacks on the line which marks the lower edge of the upholstered section.

Attaching the undercover

This undercover helps the inexperienced worker considerably. It provides practice and secures the recesses into which the buttons will fit.

5. Turn the board so that the wood is uppermost and insert two tacks at each hole, but without driving them fully into the wood. Place the calico over the foam with an equal overhang at both ends. Secure loosely with temporary tacks, making sure that the grain of the calico is always parallel to the lower edge of the wood. If the grain runs at an angle, you will find that there is no fabric to form a pleat.

6. Beginning at the centre hole, take a length of twine, twist one end round one of the two tacks and then drive this tack firmly into the wood. Thread the other end of the twine through the eye of a mattress needle and pass the needle through the hole and foam to the front of the board, then unthread the needle.

7. Return to the back of the board and pass the eye end of the needle right through, then re-thread it and draw the twine back to the wrong side of the board. Draw up the twine so that the foam is compressed and an indentation is formed. Take care when bringing the needle through the foam for the second time that it emerges a generous 1 cm (½ in) from where it emerged the first time. This reduces the risk of the twine cutting through the calico and the foam. Twist the tightened twine around the second tack and secure. Cut off the twine.

8. Turn the board so that the foam is uppermost and smooth the calico away from the button position already anchored. Keeping the grain running correctly, compress the foam where the four surrounding buttons are to be. Diagonal pleats will form. Secure these temporarily with glass-headed pins. The pleats should be facing the bottom of the board. This is particularly important when arranging the pleats in the top cover, otherwise they could become dust collectors. Secure the hollows for the buttons in these four positions. Then continue the buttoning, always moving in a diagonal direction. You may find it necessary to adjust the temporary tacks holding the edges of the calico which will tend to tighten up as you continue.

Completing the edges of the upholstery

Smoothing the calico away from the buttoning, draw it over to the back of the board and tack into position. Arrange the fullness which runs from the outside buttons in pleats. Those along the top and bottom edges should face inwards towards the centre of the board while the horizontal pleats going to the side edges must face downwards. Remove the glass-headed pins.

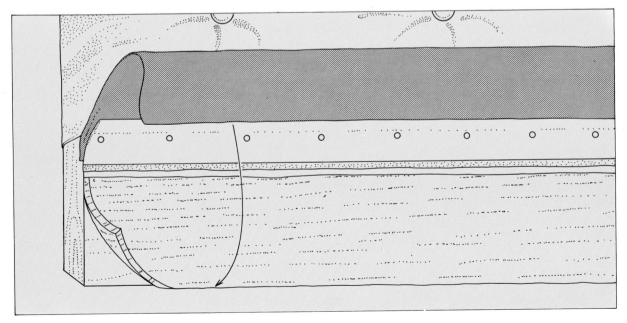

46 Back tacking ensures smooth crisp edge

*Detail of buttoned chair back with box
pleats in centre : two single pleats on top
face centre : side pleats face down*

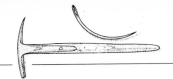

Attaching the outer cover

10. You can attach this in one of two ways:

In exactly the same way as the undercover: insert two more tacks by each hole to secure the second piece of twine, then thread the covered button on to the twine before re-threading the needle.

Mark the positions for the buttons on the covering fabric before attaching it to the headboard. If the rows of holes are 10 cm (4 in) apart, then the buttons will be further apart by a distance equal to half the thickness of the foam, i.e. 35 mm ($1\frac{1}{2}$ in) if using 75-mm (3-in) foam. The rows will be 14-18 cm ($5\frac{1}{2}$-$7\frac{1}{2}$ in) apart on the fabric. Mark their positions with tailor tacks. Increase the distance between the buttons by a similar amount, i.e. half the depth of the foam. Take care that with this method you take up all the allowance, but do not over-tighten the buttoning to produce 'waisting'. Simply use whichever method gives the best result with the greatest ease.

Finish off the edges as for the undercover and trim any spare fabric along the bottom edge, leaving about 2 cm (1 in) below the edge of the foam.

Covering the non-upholstered border

A piece of the cover material will remain after the buttoning is completed. This is large enough to cover this panel.

11. Place the right side of this piece of fabric on the buttoned surface so that the lower edge is level with the trimmed edge of the cover. Secure with a few fine tacks.

12. Cut enough strips of thin cardboard 1 cm ($\frac{1}{2}$ in) wide to stretch across the board. Place one strip on top of the lower edge of the fabric and press the edge of the cardboard up to the foam. Secure with tacks passing them through the card about 2·5 cm (1 in) apart. Check that

they are wholly on the card but as close to the foam as possible. Cut a piece of wadding to cover the visible wood and fix it with a little adhesive. Bring the cover material down over the wadding and draw to the back of the board before tacking into position (figure 46).

Note This method of attaching a strip of fabric is known as 'back tacking' and produces a clean sharp edge with no looping between adjacent tacks.

Neatening the back of the board

13. Trim away any surplus fabric from the back of the board. Cut a piece of wadding to fit over the back of the wood but allowing for a border 1 cm ($\frac{1}{2}$ in) to be left un-padded around the edge.

14. Cut a piece of lining sateen to the size of the board, plus 1 cm ($\frac{1}{2}$ in) all round. Secure the lining to the lower edge of the board with back-tacking. Then bring the lining up over the wadding and turn in 2 cm ($\frac{3}{4}$ in) on the free edges. Pin into position and, using a semicircular needle, secure with blind-stitching.

Shallow-buttoned Headboard (modern method materials)

This is a very simple form of buttoning, suitable for a room that is furnished in modern style. It is the easiest type of buttoning to use if you have chosen a vinyl covering.

You can attach the buttoning either with twine, anchored to the back of the board as in deep buttoning, or, to achieve a buttoned effect, insert enamelled studs from the front of the board and tap them through the foam into the wood. Cover the studs with a pad of wadding before hitting them with a hammer to prevent them being scratched or damaged. This shallow buttoning has the effect of creating a series of depressions.

You will need for this project:
a headboard
25-mm (1-in) polyurethane foam, 2 cm ($\frac{3}{4}$ in) larger all round than the headboard
fabric to cover the board to the size of the wood plus 5 cm (2 in) all round
calico* to the same size as the cover fabric plus enough for the strips
twine and buttons or studs
lining for the back
10-mm ($\frac{3}{8}$-in) fine tacks
adhesive

*__Note__ A calico undercover is not necessary if the top cover is vinyl.

Upholstering the headboard

1. Determine the position of the buttons and bore the holes if real buttons are to be used. It is not necessary when using 22-mm (1-in) foam to leave the lower 10 cm (4 in) non-upholstered as suggested for deep buttoning.

2. Attach the foam to the head-board as for the drop-in dining seat.

3. If you intend using a woven top cover, attach the calico undercover taking care not to over-tighten the fabric.

4. Attach the cover and complete the tacking before buttoning.

5. Position the buttons or studs, taking care, if using a vinyl cover, that the buttons do not have to be adjusted, in which case unsightly holes could be left visible on the finished work.

6. Neaten the back of the board as for the deep-buttoned headboard.

> With all foam, always make sure that it is attached to the frame with strips of calico that have had adhesive applied.
>
> Remember that latex foam cannot withstand exposure to direct light. This induces perishing. Protect the foam by a good light-proof cover.

Upholstery materials suppliers

London

Acre Upholsterers
38-40 Kennington Park Rd SE11
* John Barnes Finchley Rd NW3
Bedlam 114 Kensington Church St W8
Harry Burke 80 Leather Lane EC1
Choumert Upholsterers
131 Bellendon Rd SE15
Distinctive Trimmings
17D Kensington Church St W8
Distinctive Trimmings
11 Marylebone Lane W1
Eddies Palmerston Rd
WALTHAMSTOW E17
House of Foam 62-64 Hoe St
WALTHAMSTOW E17
W. E. Harryman 145 Half Moon
Yard HERNE HILL SE24
* Jones Brothers Holloway Rd N7
* Peter Jones Sloane Sq SW1
A. J. Kingham 42 Glenlea Rd SE9
* John Lewis Brent Cross Shopping
Centre NW4
John Lewis Oxford St W1
Norrington & Adams Lorne Close
NW3
Pentonville Rubber Co
50 Pentonville Rd N1
Plastic & Rubber Foam Supplies
39 Bargain Centre Rye Lane SE15
*Pratts Streatham High Rd
STREATHAM SW16
Russell & Chapple (Canvas &
Cordage) 23 Monmouth St WC2
Selfridges Oxford St W1
J. J. Trading Co. 76 Battersea Rise
SW11
* Trewin Brothers Queen's Rd
WATFORD
Turnross & Co. 130 Pinner Rd
HARROW
Weinsteins 86-94 Lee High Rd
SE13
Winborn Upholsterers
349 Hanworth Rd HOUNSLOW

Nationwide

Fabrics and trimmings
John Lewis Partnership stores
Enquiries: 01-629 7711
(or local store)

Dunlopillo latex foam Dunlopreme polyether foam Pirelli webbing
DIY Foams
Dunlopillo Industrial Division
Coronation Rd
HIGH WYCOMBE Bucks
Pirelli Webbing Derby Rd
BURTON-ON-TRENT Staffs
Marketing: 0283 66301

Foam
British Vita Co. Ltd.
MIDDLETON Manchester
Marketing: 061 653 6800
Product information: 061 643 1133
Booklet available: 'Foam for all reasons'

Traditional materials
(Hessians, twill, duck, canvas, twines)
Russell & Chapple
23 Monmouth St
LONDON WC2
Tel: 01-836 7521

Foam mail order Spa Foam Ltd.
Melbourne St LEEDS Yorks
Enquiries: 0532 30824

Books for further reference

Upholstery: a Step-by-step Guide, Jeanne Argent, Hamlyn, 1974
Mending and Restoring Furniture, J. W. Collier and G. Dixon, Garnstone, 1972
Modern Upholstery, Dorothy Cox, Bell & Hyman, 1970
Do Your Own Upholstery, Dena Cross, Foulsham, 1975
Upholstery, M. Flitman, Batsford, 1972
Practical Upholstery, C. Howes, Evans Bros., 1950 (latest edition 1977)
Upholstery Repair and Restoration, R. J. MacDonald, Batsford, 1977
Mending and Restoring Upholstery and Soft Furnishings, W. Morton and N. Richardson, Garnstone, 1973
Soft Furnishings: a Practical Introduction, Joanne Prior, Bell & Hyman, 1970

* Fabrics and trimmings only

This list of suppliers is offered merely as an aid to purchasers. It is not comprehensive, but to the publishers' knowledge the details are correct at the time of publishing. WI Books Ltd and the publishers cannot accept responsibility for the accuracy of the information.

Dress your rooms with colour

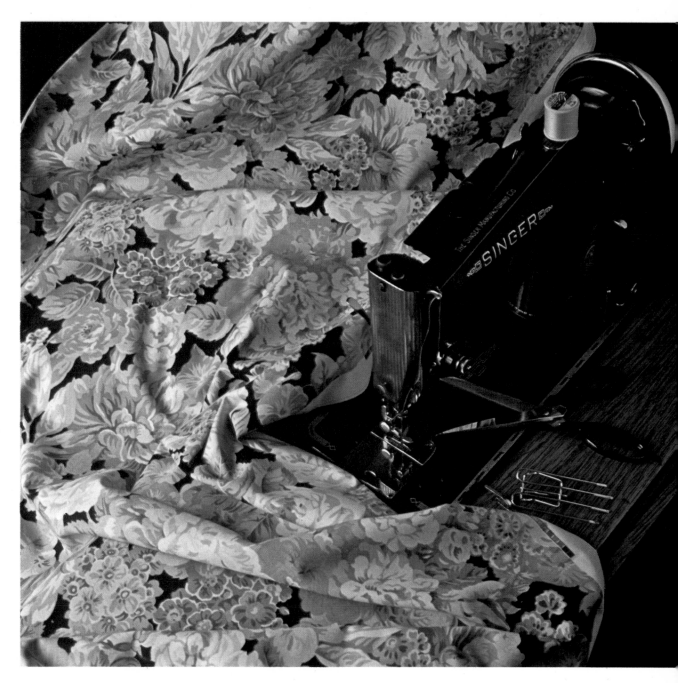

If not quite all the little things in life are free, at least you can freely imprint your own taste on those little things that help to make a home comfortable. Cushions, curtains and quilts can give your rooms a colourful background that suits your intimate moods and proclaims your domestic lifestyle. You will find the making of them as satisfying as the finished results, and if you take note of the professional tips in the pages that follow, those results should be first-class.

Making Cushions

Cushion-making is well within the scope of the average needlewoman. Cushions are simple to make and will give new life to a weary scheme at very little expense. They not only add comfort, but can be used to reinforce the main colour scheme in the room or supply a note of contrast.

Because fashion plays such an increasingly important role in our everyday needs, the style of cushions has changed as has that of other household furnishings. Low chunky sofas have made the smaller scatter cushion very popular. In contrast, large, soft cushions have made their way on to the floor, to suit today's more informal lifestyles.

In choosing cushions there are various factors to consider, such as the style of furniture they are to adorn, the other soft furnishings in the room and the type of wear to which they will be subjected.

Consider all the soft furnishings in a room as a connected scheme for a balance of colour and pattern. Plain cushions will look good on a multi-coloured suite; patterned ones best on a plain chair or sofa. Take your ideas for colours from the furniture rather than the other way round. Pick the colours from a patterned fabric for a range of small, plain scatter cushions, or choose a pretty or boldly patterned fabric to give interest to a plain background. For many years, cushions tended to be one colour only but fashion now allows us to break such a rule and experiment at will. Do not forget curtains, for these can be linked either to the suite itself, or to the fabric or fabrics used for cushion covers.

There are usually three separate parts to a cushion:
(a) the filling, which provides the comfort;

(b) the pad cover, which contains and controls the filling;
(c) the outer cover—decorative in texture, shape or pattern.

Fillings

There are various types, including curled poultry feathers, feather and down mixtures, wool flock, sheet foam, foam chippings, and Terylene floss filling. Kapok is rarely used nowadays. It very quickly becomes lumpy in use, making the cushion shapeless. It has been replaced, very successfully, by Terylene floss. This, by the way, is recommended for anyone allergic to feathers, or when a completely washable cushion is required (in a nursery, for instance).

Feather or feather and down filling provides a very comfortable cushion and one which is easy to keep in a good shape. Wool flock and sheet foam are both suitable for making mattress or squab cushions as they give a tailored outline. This makes them perfect for cushions fitted on a particular chair or seat. Chip foam is suitable for garden and beach cushions, as it is not affected by damp in the way that other fillings are.

Inner Cases for Cushions

It is best not to make a cushion by stuffing the outer cover directly, because of the laundering difficulties. Make a separate pad cover from a suitably strong material to contain the filling. The choice of fabric is determined by the type of filling you intend to use.

A down-proof cotton is best for a feather or hair filling. This is a finely woven material, specially treated or 'proofed' to prevent the filling escaping. Take the following precautions, however, when using such material.
(a) Pin and tack in the seam allowance only to prevent puncturing

(Left) Inner and outer covers

(Above) Outer cover of unboxed cushion

the fabric in any other place.
(b) Use a fine machine needle and a very small stitch. Double-stitch all seams.
(c) Wax the finished seam on both sides with beeswax or a candle to prevent the filling escaping.
(d) Most down-proof fabrics have a shiny and a dull side. Check before stitching that the shiny side will be

inside the finished pad and so be in contact with the feathers.

Make an inner cover of firm, closely woven fabric such as unbleached calico to contain foam fillings. This will help to exclude the light which destroys foam.

If you want a Terylene filling, make the pad cover from a Terylene or polyester fabric so that the whole pad can be washed easily.

The Outer Cover

You have a wide choice here, ranging from linens to velvets, and from brocade to hand-embroidered fabrics. Consider where and how often the cushion will be used, and check whether the fabric can be washed or has to be dry-cleaned. Also, if it is not shrink-proof, allow for shrinkage.

Unboxed Cushion (without gusset)

An unboxed cushion looks better if it is square or rectangular. Circular cushions tend to develop undulating edges and they are better 'boxed' with the addition of a gusset.

For a really professional finish, the pad should completely fill the cover, reaching the seams and extending right into the corners. To achieve this, cut the pad 2·5 cm (1 in) *larger* than the cover. In addition, allow 1-cm ($\frac{1}{2}$-in) turnings on all seams. Here are some basic measurements:

Cushion finished	Cover cut
46 x 46 cm	48 x 48 cm
(18 x 18 in)	(19 x 19 in)
40 x 56 cm	43 x 58 cm
(16 x 22 in)	(17 x 23 in)
Pad finished	Pad cut
48 x 48 cm	50 x 50 cm
(19 x 19 in)	(20 x 20 in)
43 x 58 cm	46 x 60 cm
(17 x 23 in)	(18 x 24 in)

Cushions intended to appear square or rectangular when finished very often have protruding or 'butterfly' corners. To prevent this, reduce the pattern by 1 cm ($\frac{1}{2}$ in) on each corner tapering in 8 cm (3 in).

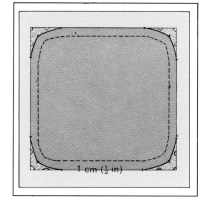

1 *Reduced corners*

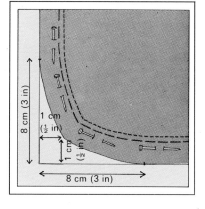

2 *Pattern for reduced corner*

(Left) Soft unboxed velvet cushion with canvas-work central panel
(Above) Soft unboxed tie-dye cushion; reduced corners give squared finish

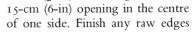

Cutting out and making up the inner cover

1. Decide the size of the completed cushion, e.g. 46 x 46 cm (18 x 18 in). (Make adjustment for other sizes.)
2. Add the necessary allowances for the pad, i.e. 4 cm (2 in).
3. Cut a paper pattern measuring 50 x 50 cm (20 x 20 in).
4. Reduce corners (figures 1, 2).
5. Pin the pattern to the fabric chosen for the pad cover. If this fabric is down-proof, keep the pins within the seam allowance.

Note Avoid making holes through which filling can escape:
6. Cut out two identical pieces.
7. Pin these pieces together, right sides facing, so that the glazed sides are outside.
8. Tack along the seam allowance and stitch along the seamline, i.e. 1 cm ($\frac{1}{2}$ in) from edge. Leave a 15-cm (6-in) opening in the centre of one side. Finish any raw edges

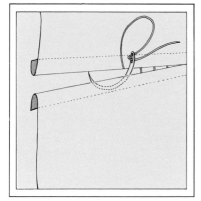

3 Blind stitching

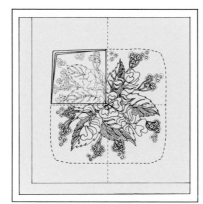

4 Positioning pattern on flowered fabric

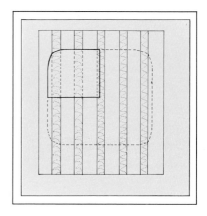

5 Positioning pattern on striped fabric

with zigzag stitching or a second row of straight stitching.

9. Wax over the machine stitching and seam allowances, then turn the cover to the right side.

10. Insert filling so that the pad is soft to the pressure of the hand, but full enough to maintain its shape when supported on the fingers of one hand. It should not be necessary to shake the cushion after use to retain its shape.

11. Close the opening with blind stitching (figure 3).

Cutting out and making up the outer cover

1. Reduce the paper pattern by 1 cm ($\frac{1}{2}$ in) all round—the shape retaining the outline of the reduced corners.

2. When placing the pattern on striped or patterned fabric care must be taken to balance the design or centralize a motif (figures 4, 5).

3. Pin the pattern on to the wrong side of the fabric and cut two identical pieces.

Note It is safer to cut these one at a time to ensure the grain and pattern coincide.

4. Mark the stitching line with chalk or tacking stitches 1 cm ($\frac{1}{2}$ in) from the cut edge. Use this line when attaching edging.

5. Select the type of edging—piping or trimming—and position around one section of the cover. Pin to the right side and tack along the stitching line. Place the second section over the first, right sides facing, so that the edging is between the two layers of fabric, then pin and tack. Machine-stitch 1 cm ($\frac{1}{2}$ in) from the edge. Leave an opening of 30 cm (12 in) in the centre of one side edge of the cushion (the bottom edge if the cushion is oblong or patterned).

Boxed cushion with printed eastern panels and birds; in this instance the shape and size of the cushion were determined by the design of the panels and the decoration of the fabric; note very fine piped edging

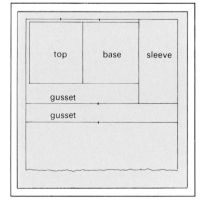

6 *Cutting plan for box cushion*

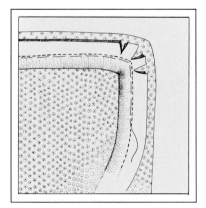

7 *Cornering piping cord*

Square or Rectangular Boxed Cushion (with gusset)

Boxed cushions are often regarded as being difficult to make. The two major faults that can occur in them are twisted corners and an uneven gusset or box. By paying particular attention to these two details, you can overcome the problems.

First, slash the corners of the box very carefully. Secondly, work slowly when attaching the box to the two main cushion sections so that tacking line matches tacking line as accurately as possible.

Cutting out cover and pad

1. Cut a paper pattern to the size of the completed pad, plus 1 cm (½ in) seam allowances.
2. Pin the pattern on the wrong side of the fabric, centralizing the motif or stripe if necessary. Cut out and mark the stitching line with chalk or pencil 1 cm (½ in) from the edges. Cut a second section to match.
3. Cut pieces of fabric to measure right round the box, plus seam allowances for joining into one long strip. Cut the length of the strips for the box or gusset across the width of the fabric—i.e. from selvedge to selvedge. Make these

strips 2·5 cm (1 in) wider than the finished depth of cushion, so allowing 1 cm (½ in) turning on the top and bottom edge. See the cutting plan (figure 6).
4. Cut crossway strips measuring 2·5-4 cm (1¼-1½ in) wide to cover the piping cord and edges.
5. Prepare the piping cord.
6. Join the sections of the box into one long strip and mark or tack stitching lines 1 cm (½ in) from each cut edge. If the material is liable to fray, machine on the stitching line with a very small stitch. This will act as a barrier against fraying when the corners are slashed.
7. Fit the piping round the top side of the cushion, pinning to the right side of the fabric. Insert each pin on the tacking line and pass as close to the cord as possible. Then slash the piping covering at the corners to avoid puckering (figure 7). Tack into position and join the ends neatly (figure 8). Pipe in a similar fashion round the bottom section of the cushion.
8. Pin the box to the top piped edge of the cushion, right sides facing, as follows. Slash the box at the first corner, right up to the tacking line marked with an X (figure 9). Repeat at the other three corners, then tack all round. The slash in the seam allowance opens to form an 'L' at each corner, so preventing any fullness appearing on the completed cushion.

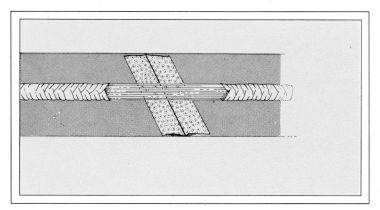

8 *Joining crossway strip and cord to give invisible join*

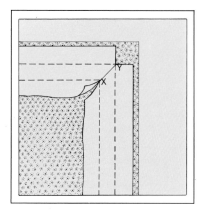

9 *Slash box at corner*

9. Pin the bottom edge of the cushion to the box, fitting the four corners first, matching the first corner to point Y. This prevents twisted corners. After the four corners are matched, fit the fabric in between. Tack it in place.

Note It is easier to work this fitting on a flat surface.

10. Stitch all round using a zipper or piping foot. Leave an opening along the lower edge at the back of cushion to be closed with a zip or Velcro.

Making the pad

Cut and assemble in exactly the same way as for the cover, without piping the seams joining the box to the top and the bottom sections of the cushion.

Note Unlike an unboxed cushion, the pad and the outer cover are cut to the same size and no reduction is made at the corners. If the cushion is to be filled with a feather mixture, make the pad from down-proof cambric. Similarly, if the filling is to be foam, make the cover of a closely woven unbleached calico.

To make a foam pad, use the same pattern as for the top and bottom sections of the cover. Take care when cutting the foam that the pair of scissors or knife is held absolutely vertical to give a straight firm edge to the pad.

A more attractive-looking cushion results from cutting the pad in two sections, each being half the depth of the finished cushion: for example, two layers of 50-mm (2-in) foam to give a 100-mm (4-in) cushion. Then cut a piece of 25-mm (1-in) foam to measure 5-7 cm (2-3 in) smaller than the two sections. Place this in between the larger pieces of foam and glue the three layers together with upholstery adhesive. Great care must be taken that the doming is placed centrally (figures 10, 11).

(Above) Humpty and cushion, both made as boxed cushions: the box of the base is 25 cm (9 in) deep and that of the cushion 8 cm (3 in) deep; the pattern is identical on all four sides, and all covers can easily be removed for laundering as required; note the tautness of the covers and the squareness of the corners

(Right) Circular boxed cushion showing evenness of gusset and the double-piped edging; see also piped edging on cushions over page

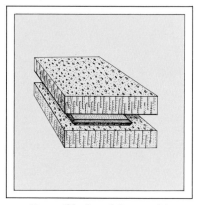

11 *Reversible domed foam cushion*

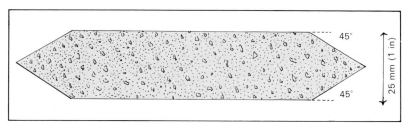

Cross-section of doming, showing feathering

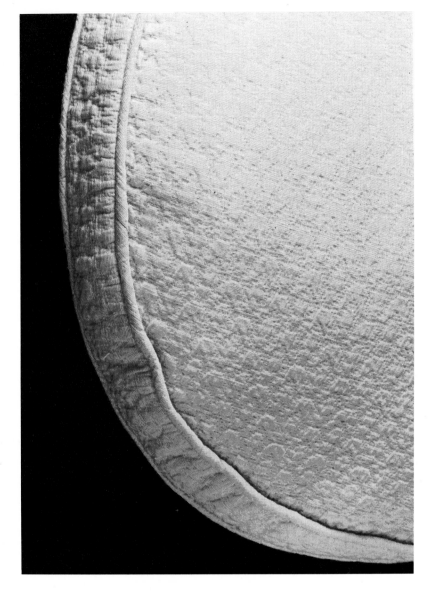

Circular Boxed Cushion (with gusset)

This is a fairly easy style to make up, but take particular care that the gusset does not become twisted.

1. Cut two circles of fabric to make the pad the size of the finished cushion, plus 1 cm ($\frac{1}{2}$ in) for seam allowances (figure 12).

2. Cut a strip (or strips) for the gusset measuring 5-7 cm (2-3 in) wide x the circumference of the circle. Allow 1 cm ($\frac{1}{2}$ in) on both edges and ends for seam allowances.

3. Mark the stitching lines with chalk or pencil on the wrong side of the circles and gusset, 1 cm ($\frac{1}{2}$ in) from cut edges.

4. Carefully slash the seam allowances on the gusset to stitching lines on both edges to allow for smooth fit (figure 13).

5. On the circles (figure 12), mark halves and quarters A, B, C, D and A′, B′, C′ and D′.

6. With unglazed right sides facing, place the gusset strip round the edge of one circle. Stitch the short ends of the gusset and trim away any excess fabric (figure 14).

Note The slashes will open when the gusset is stitched to the fabric and create an even seam.

7. Fit the top of cushion A′ over A, B′ over B etc (figure 12). Then fit the intervening fabric section by section. This is *very* important,

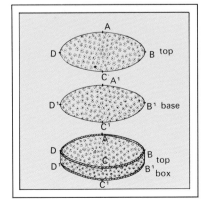

12 Assembling circular boxed cushion

13 Slash seam allowances on gusset

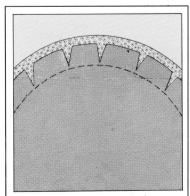

14 Fitting gusset

otherwise the gusset could be twisted.

8. Tack and stitch, leaving an opening for filling. Machine along the stitching line exactly to give a really smooth seam.

9. Turn and fill as for previous cushion.

Making the cover

Make this in the same way, but pipe the seams.

Decorative Edgings for Cushions

These give a professional, neat and attractive finish to a cushion. Consider the texture and nature of the fabric when deciding what type of edging to use. Ruches and gathers are suitable for soft fabric, while piping and pleating are more suitable for thicker fabrics and linens. Piped edges are most suitable for boxed cushions with a gusset, and all forms of quilting.

Piped edgings

Piping cord can be bought in various thicknesses. If it is cotton, boil before use. This prevents shrinkage during laundering or dry-cleaning. Nylon cord does not need to be boiled and, because it has a smooth surface, it is less liable to wear through the covering fabric.

The cord is covered with strips of fabric cut on the true cross. For small articles, such as a cushion, sufficient piping can be cut in strips; for larger articles, it is more practical to make a sleeve.

For fine cord, cut the strips 3 cm ($1\frac{1}{4}$ in) wide; with coarser cords or fabric that frays, cut the strips 4-5 cm ($1\frac{1}{4}$-2 in) wide.

Join cotton piping cord by splicing and staggering the joins of the three different plies by 1 cm ($\frac{1}{2}$ in) for an invisible and smooth join. Cut synthetic cord with sloping edges and then join the two edges with a spot of clear adhesive.

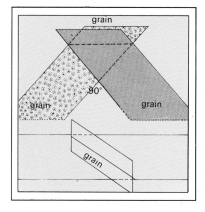

15 *Joining single crossway strips*

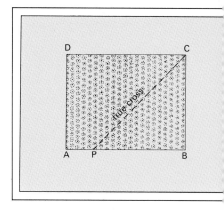

16 *Making sleeve for continuous piping*

Joining single crossway strips

Join crossway or bias-cut strips on the straight of the thread or grain (figure 15). Place two strips together, right sides facing, over-lapping to form a V shape at points A and B (figure 15). The stitching *must* run between these two points for a perfect join.

Open out the small seam and press. Machine tack piping cord into the binding before use. Set your machine to a large stitch, then fix the cord into the casing using the zipper foot and the large stitch. This stitching acts as a barrier against fraying when the material is slashed.

Making a sleeve for a piped edging

This is a method of producing a long strip of crossway fabric which

Candlewick cushions trimmed with cotton-bobble edging, cotton fringing

is simple to use and saves a great deal of time.

1. To begin, cut a perfect rectangle of fabric. It should follow the thread or grain of the fabric and measure not less than 22 cm (9 in) wide.

2. Cut off the bottom right-hand corner (BCP) of the strip on the true cross (figure 16).

3. Slide the cut triangle marked BCP to the opposite end of the rectangle to form a parallelogram. Pin the two pieces of material together—the seam marked A-D being a single seam—and machine with very small stitches. Press the seam open (figure 17).

4. Draw a line X-Y—the required width from B-P. Do not cut off.

5. Fold the fabric as shown in figure 18, matching the long edges but marking point P as being taken

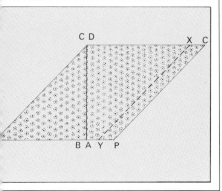

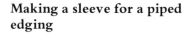

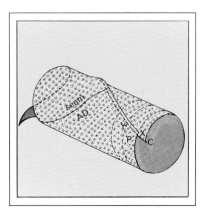

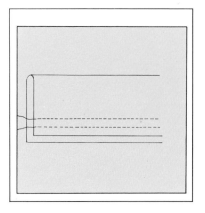

17 Form parallelogram

18 Fold, match long edges, stitch seam

19 Frilled edging

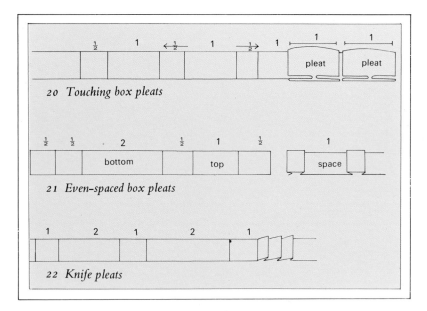

20 *Touching box pleats*

21 *Even-spaced box pleats*

22 *Knife pleats*

The pattern on the fabric has been carefully used to give a balanced appearance to the made-up cushions

to point X. Tack and stitch the seam.

6. Cut along the line X-Y and then continue cutting, keeping the strip a uniform width (figure 18).

Frilled edging

This type of edging is best made from any soft fabric such as tussore or crêpe. Cut a strip 8 cm (3 in) wide and allow twice the perimeter measurement of the cushion for fullness. Fold down the centre with the wrong sides facing. Machine two rows of gathering stitches, the first 2 cm ($\frac{3}{4}$ in) from the raw edge, the second 1 cm ($\frac{1}{2}$ in) from the first row of stitching. Two rows of gathering prevent the frill from twisting. Distribute the fullness evenly around the edge of the cushion (figure 19).

Ruched edging

Make this in the same way as the frilled edging but cut the strips 5-6 cm (2-2$\frac{1}{2}$ in) wide, then folded over a soft piping cord. The result is a ruched piping.

Pleated edging

This type of edging is suitable for all linen-type fabrics. Cut 8-9 cm (3-3$\frac{1}{2}$ in) strips and fold lengthways to use. It is a rather expensive type of edging, using rather a lot of fabric, but is successful in small areas—down the short edges of rectangular cushions, for example.

Touching box pleats Allow three times the perimeter measurement of the cushion (figure 20).

Even-spaced box pleats Allow twice the perimeter measurement (figure 21).

Knife pleats Allow three times the perimeter measurement (figure 22).

Methods of Closing Cushion Covers

Removing a cover for laundering need no longer be a time-consuming chore. Very neat openings result from using either a zip fastener or Velcro.

Inserting a zip fastener

1. Open the zip and place the right side of the zip to the right side of the cover, the edge of the tape to the raw edge of the cover. The teeth should now lie exactly on the stitching line. Tack and stitch in place using a piping or zipper foot (figure 23).

2. Fold the front of the cushion so that the edge of the fold line lies over the edge of the teeth, back-stitch in place with a stabbing motion (figure 24).

3. Attach the opposite side of the zip in the same way.

4. Over-stitch the edge of the tape to the edge of the cushion; this prevents jamming when the cover is in use. Secure the ends of the tapes to the seam allowance at each end of the fastener with a few neat stitches worked by hand.

Applying Velcro

Note This product should not be used on an edge neatened with a

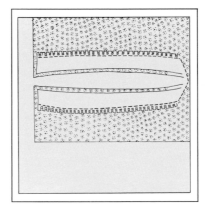

23 *Inserting a zip*

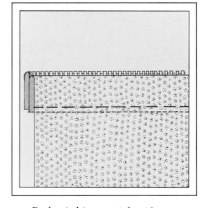

24 *Back stitching on right side*

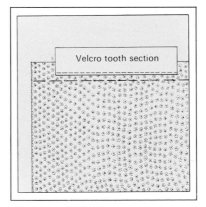

25 *Attaching Velcro tooth section to the bottom of the cushion on the right side*

Velcro tooth section

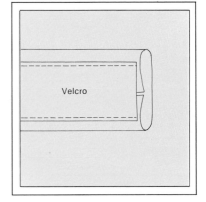

26 *Slip stitching the Velcro tooth section on the wrong side*

Velcro

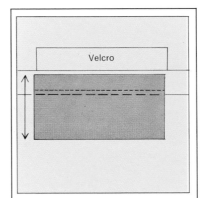

27 *Attaching Velcro velvet section to the top of the cushion on the wrong side*

Velcro

28 *Stitch edges together on the right side*

Velcro

commercial tassel or fringe.

1. Separate the two sections of Velcro.

2. Position one half on the right side of the *bottom* of the cushion just inside the stitching line, tack and stitch (figure 25).

3. Fold over to the wrong side of the fabric and slip-stitch to the inside of the cover (figure 26).

4. Repeat stage 2 with the other half of the Velcro, but attaching it to the right side of the *top* of the cushion.

5. Cut or tear a strip of thin fabric to face this edge equal to the length of the Velcro but twice as wide. Place the right side of this strip to the wrong side of the cushion, matching the edge of the strip to the edge of the cushion. Stitch along the seam line of the cushion (figure 27). Fold the strip for-ward, turn in the raw edge so that the folded edge comes to the edge of the Velcro, then stitch these edges together (figure 28). Over-sew the ends of the two sections of Velcro together by hand.

Making Curtains

Curtains are an important feature in the furnishing scheme of any room. They affect both appearance and character, and usually have to last several years. It is very important to choose a fabric with care, so look around first before making a final decision. For curtains to be effective, take the following factors into consideration:

(a) the balance of pattern in the room;

(b) the type of windows—bow, casement, picture, etc.;

(c) the size of the window in relation to the room;

(d) the atmosphere created by the view through the window;

(e) the type of room—bedroom, living room, etc.;

(f) the orientation of the window;

(g) the amount of money available.

The range of fabrics available, in terms of texture, weight, design and cost, is enormous. Many beautifully designed fabrics are available, but if you already have a striking pattern in the room, settle for plain curtains which complement and emphasize the colour and design of the carpet, walls or furniture.

Curtains can be used to minimize or even remedy faults in a room. If windows are very small, you can make them appear larger by carrying the curtain beyond the frame on either side. Full-length curtains will add emphasis to an ordinary window, while short curtains tend to unbalance a large sash window.

Fabrics

Curtains are usually made from cotton, linen, rayon, man-made fibres or various combinations of fibres. Net curtains are usually of cotton or Terylene.

Natural fibres present their own problems, but each has its own assets. Cotton is comparatively inexpensive but, though easy to care for, tends to shrink considerably when washed. Linen does not shrink to the same degree but is more expensive. A mix of these two fibres results in a very practical fabric. Rayon combined with cotton creates a fabric which drapes most gracefully; however, it does present laundering difficulties, as rayon weakens when wet. Some very attractive brocades are made from a combination of rayon and cotton, but these are not usually suitable for washing. The modern fabrics made from man-made fibres launder excellently if washed with

would need one and a half times the width of the track for heavy fabric or twice the width for net curtains. This is now considered old-fashioned, besides which there are other factors to be taken into account.

(a) The width of window and track.

(b) The texture of fabric—there are now many coarse open-weave fabrics which form the actual curtain and up to three times the width may be needed.

(c) Type of heading available. There are many tapes available, e.g. standard, deep pleat, pinch pleat, cartridge pleat. With some tapes, the amount of fullness may have to be exact when no adjustment is possible. Check the width of the finished curtain before buying the heading tape.

(d) If using a patterned fabric, the depth of the repeat of the pattern. The pattern should be continuous and unbroken across the window. It is usual to allow one extra pattern repeat for each length of fabric after the first.

(e) The depth of the lower hem. Allow 15-20 cm (6-8 in) for a floor-length curtain and 10-15 cm (4-6 in) for short curtains to the level of the sill. The hem of sheer nets should always be of three thicknesses, the first turning being equal to the depth of the finished hem.

(f) Allow 1-10 cm ($\frac{1}{2}$-4 in) at the top of the curtain, depending on the choice of heading or tape.

Treatment of Selvedges

The treatment of selvedges often reveals the hand of an amateur curtain-maker. Do give sufficient thought to the problems presented by the more concentrated weave at the edges of the fabric.

Curtains made from natural fibres need special care at the edges, unless the fabric is guaranteed shrinkproof. As the selvedges are more densely woven, they tend to shrink more when washed. The result is that when the curtain is re-hung the selvedges pucker and the hem rises at the sides. To combat this, trim or slash the selvedges.

Fabrics made from man-made fibres fortunately do not need this drastic treatment. You will find that the treatment of the edges will vary according to the texture and weave of the fabric. In some you can leave the edges in their natural state. On other types, it may only be necessary to turn back a single layer of fabric. Edges that have printing running down the selvedges present another problem. Either cut them away or turn them in to form the first turning of a double hem so that they are hidden.

Side hems should be between 1-2 cm ($\frac{1}{2}$-$\frac{3}{4}$ in) wide. These are best sewn down by hand, but the lengths and number of curtains used at modern windows tend to make this rather impractical. If your sewing machine has a swing-needle, stitching can be almost invisible—particularly on some textured fabrics. If the machine has a blind hemming attachment and disc, use them. Test the stitch and swing on a sample of fabric before starting to work on the curtains.

Velvet curtains hang best with padded hems. Secure a narrow strip of Terylene wadding 5-8 cm (2-3 in) wide with herringbone stitch down each side of the curtain an equal distance from the edge of the fabric. Then roll back the unwadded border and herringbone into position. This gives an attractive rolled edge to the curtain and helps to prevent the pile wearing away.

If your curtains look like the one shown here, these pages will certainly help you to put matters right. Don't you long to replace your old ones? Remember that quite apart from the fun you will have in making things for yourself it is always cheaper—and infinitely more satisfying

care. Use cool water and never over-spin.

Quantities of Fabric

These need to be very carefully calculated.

There used to be a very simple rule which stipulated that you

Joining Widths of Curtain Together

If incorporating more than one width of fabric into a curtain, use one of three seams:
(a) a machine and fell seam for unlined curtains;
(b) a flat seam for lined curtains;
(c) a French seam 3 mm ($\frac{1}{8}$ in) wide for sheer nets.

Machine and fell seam

Place the right sides of the fabric together, slashing or removing the selvedges if necessary, then match the pattern. Tack 1 cm ($\frac{1}{2}$ in) from the edge and stitch. Trim away one edge to 3 mm ($\frac{1}{8}$ in) (figure 1) and bring both raw edges down so that the trimmed edge is covered. Turn in the raw edge of the wider turning and stitch down into position (figures 2, 3).

Flat seam

Begin this as for the machine and fell seam, but after stitching the two sections together, press the seam open, with no trimming on either side (figure 4).

(Right) Detail of curtain made from one whole width and one half width, with pattern carefully matched, as in figures 7, 8; (Far right) Lined cotton curtain hung from pinch-pleat heading

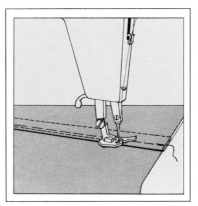

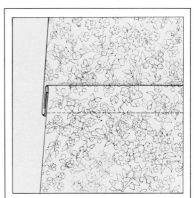

1 Trim one edge, machine and fell seam   *2 Stitch on wrong side*   *3 Right side*

French seam

Begin by placing both wrong sides together, then stitch these 5 mm ($\frac{1}{4}$ in) from the edge and trim the turning to 3 mm ($\frac{1}{8}$ in). Open the seam and fold the fabric back so that the right sides are facing. Stitch the seam 5 mm ($\frac{1}{4}$ in) from the edge so that the raw edges are trapped inside the hem (figures 5, 6).

Matching Patterns

It is not easy to try to match from the wrong side of the fabric, so follow this easy method:
1. Place one width of fabric on a flat surface, right side uppermost.
2. Fold under a turning on the second width and place this over the edge of the first width (second width right side uppermost). You can then match the pattern with ease (figure 7).
3. Blind tack with matching thread.
4. Open out the fabrics (right sides facing) and stitch along the tacking stitches.

Note Now that very wide windows are common in modern homes and a generous fullness is fashionable in all curtains, a great many widths of fabric normally have to be used. To make the curtains easier to handle when laundering, they are frequently made up in single widths.

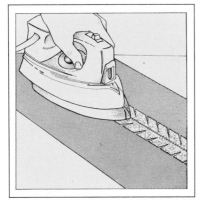

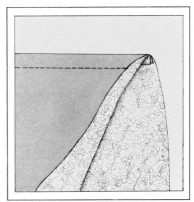

4 *Flat seam, press seam open*

5 *French seam, stitch and trim*

6 *Stitch trapping edges inside*

Using Half-widths

These are still used for smaller windows, especially when a very heavy and expensive fabric is featured. Attach the half-widths so they are at the outer edge of the window (figure 8).

Unlined Curtains

These are quick and easy to make; lightweight fabrics such as cotton or an open-weave fabric are most suitable. More expensive fabrics may require lining, for a number of reasons: to extend the curtains' life, to improve the hang or to make them thicker so that they keep out the light more effectively. The following techniques also apply to the construction of lined curtains.

Choosing a heading

A wide range of headings is available. Pelmets and frills have been less fashionable in recent years, particularly in modern homes. If you do favour a pelmet, however, use a standard tape. This is usually about 2·5 cm (1 in) wide, has two draw strings and pockets into which the hooks are inserted. Standard tape is generally available in a range of colours.

(Right) Open-weave Dralon curtain suspended by deep-pleat tape attached to heading that gives a pleasant, densely-folded fall to the curtains when open and an effective pleated fullness when drawn; no finish was required at the edge of the fabric because of the self-neatening type of weave, the weight of the bottom hem produces an attractive fall (Far right) Light-weight curtain of Swedish cotton; the selvedges were slashed to prevent puckering and a narrow double hem of 1 cm (½ in) was machine-stitched with a blind hemmer; for the attachment of standard, pencil-pleat and pinch-pleat tape to headings, see figures 9, 10 and 11

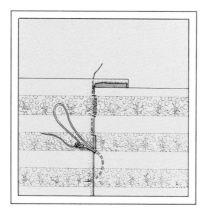

7 *Matching patterns*

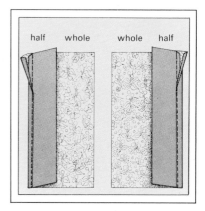

8 *Using half-widths*

Pencil pleating

This tape is 9 cm (3½ in) wide. It may be of cotton or a man-made fibre. Standard tape has a built-in filament which strengthens the tape and produces a crisp erect pleat. Take care when using these tapes to attach them the correct way up. If the track is attached to the wall, the pockets should be at the bottom of the tape. But if the track is attached to the ceiling, place the pocket edge of the tape at the top of the curtain. For this type of tape, allow widths of curtaining equal to 2½–3 times the length of the track. Make a top turning of 1 cm (½ in) only and fix the tape to within 3 mm (⅛ in) of the top of the curtain.

Pinch pleats

This tape results in a very attractive form of triple pleating. It is important to buy the type of tape suitable for the position of the track, so check at time of purchase. Attach in the same way as for the pencil-pleat tape. Width allowance is usually twice the width of the track.

Note It is important to use a tape of man-made fibre on man-made fabrics so that tape and fabric dry at the same speed.

Attaching the heading
(using a standard tape 2·5 cm/1 in wide)

With this type of tape, it is usual to have a heading above the tape, usually about 2·5 cm (1 in) in depth. Any deeper heading will require stiffening to make it stand erect.
1. Turn down a single turning of 4 cm (1½ in) to the wrong side of the fabric—the fold being along the straight of the grain or threads; then pin and tack in place.
2. Draw out the cords from one end of the tape to leave a turning of 2·5 cm (1 in). Tie the two ends together with a reef knot. Turn under the allowance and place the tape at the top of the curtain on

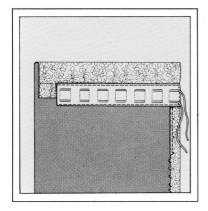

9 *Standard tape*

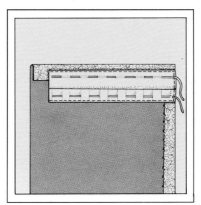

10 *Pencil pleat tape*

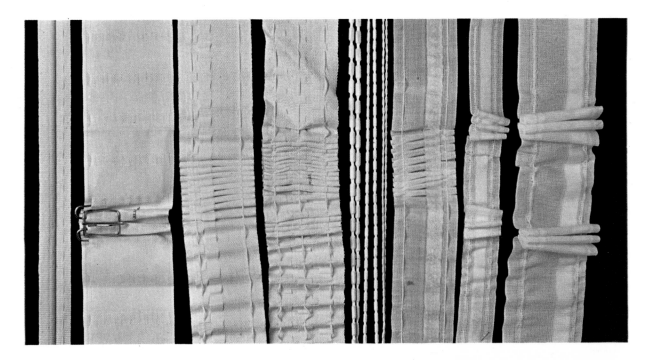

A selection of curtain tapes for headings with some commercial weights for bottom hems; for normal-weight curtains, standard, pinch-pleat with clip, pencil-pleat tapes; heavy, medium and light commercial weights for bottom hems; for lighter fabrics, pencil-pleat, standard and pinch-pleat synthetic tapes

the wrong side, 2·5 cm (1 in) below the top fold. Tack securely into position.

3. With the bulk of the curtain to the left of the machine, stitch along the top edge of the tape. Cut off the threads. Stitch the other side of the tape in similar way, but include both short ends in this row.

Note To control a very large

curtain under the arm of the machine is difficult.

4. Draw up the curtain by pulling the free cords together for an even pleating. Then tie the free ends in a neat bow so that they will be out of sight.

5. Make up a second curtain in the same way, but knotting the ends at the opposite side (figure 9).

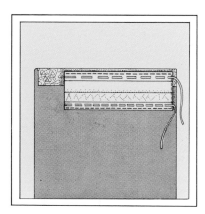

11 Pinch pleat tape

Hints

Use a tape of man-made fibre on man-made fabrics—so that in laundering tape and fabric will dry at the same speed.

Keep the bulk of fabric to the left of machine, as you will find it is difficult to control a large curtain under the arm of your sewing machine.

Turn up the bottom hem when you have hung the curtain. Leave for a few days before tacking and finishing off.

Two examples of gathering using pinch-pleat tape and clips

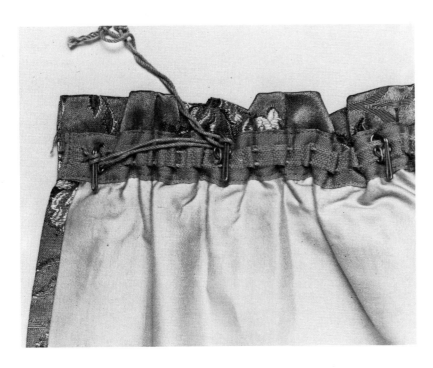

Pencil pleats

Attach and stitch in the same way
but with the heading within 3 mm
($\frac{1}{8}$ in) of the top edge of the curtain
(figure 10).

Pinch pleats

Attach in a similar position to the
pencil pleating but set back the
first set of pleats from the inner edge
of the curtain by a distance equal to
half that between the set of pleats
(figure 11).

Neatening lower hems

Turn up the hem when the curtain
is in position. Ideally, leave the
curtain hanging a few days before
finally neatening the lower edge.
Pin and tack the hem before stitching by hand or machine.
Note Stitch by hand preferably,
unless your machine has a blind
hemmer attachment.

   Some curtain hems can be very
successfully anchored with iron-on
tape. These will withstand washing
perfectly well, as long as you
follow the manufacturer's instructions to the letter.

Lined Curtains

These are more expensive and
troublesome to make than unlined
ones, but have certain advantages.
(a) They make the curtains impossible to see through.
(b) They improve the hang, sup-
port the curtain fabric and give a
softly rounded effect to the fold.
(c) They protect the fabric against
the effect of sunlight, which can rot
and fade the fibres. If all curtains
are lined alike, a uniform appearance
from outside the house is ensured.
(d) They protect the fabric by
absorbing much of the dirt and
chemicals which would otherwise
settle in the curtains themselves,
thus shortening their life.
(e) They provide additional warmth
by excluding draughts.

   To make laundering easier,
linings are often made so that they
are detachable. This means that
you can wash them more frequently
than the curtains if necessary. Lining
sateen can be bought in a variety of
colours, but the common cream
cotton lining is usually cheaper than
coloured lining material.
Note Lined curtains are not as
popular as they used to be because
of the increasingly common use of
central heating.

Size of lining

Make the lining so that it is one and
a half times the width of the finished
curtain, even though the curtain
may have greater fullness. It should
be 2·5 cm (1 in) shorter after attachment.

Making a detachable lining

1. Slash the selvedge of the lining
and work a 1-cm ($\frac{1}{2}$-in) double hem
down each long edge.
2. Cut the lining heading tape
2·5 cm (1 in) longer than the lining
width. Draw the cords 1 cm ($\frac{1}{2}$ in)
from each end of the tape and knot
them at one end.
3. Open out the 'Y' section of the
tape working with the corded side
uppermost (the upper lip is slightly
shorter than the underlip). Slip the

top edge of the lining between the two lips and tack.

4. Fold over the excess tape to the wrong side of the lining at each end and tack in place.

5. Stitch along the lower edge of the top lip (corded side uppermost).

Attaching the lining

1. Draw up the curtain to the required width.

2. Draw up the lining so that it is 2·5 cm (1 in) narrower than the curtain.

3. Slot a hook through the extreme end pocket of the curtain tape.

4. Slot the next hook through the end pocket of lining tape and into the second pocket of the curtain tape. Join the edges of curtain and lining at the hem level with a piece of Velcro at each side.

Making attached linings

Curtains with this type of lining usually need to be dry-cleaned on account of their bulk and weight. However, many people consider that the bulk and weight of attached linings cause curtains to hang more gracefully.

Cut the linings as carefully and accurately as the curtains themselves so as to ensure a perfect square edge. You can, however, cut them shorter than the 'cut' size of the curtains so that the hem is hidden on the inside. Cut them 8 cm (3 in) narrower than the finished width of the curtains if working a 4-cm (1½-in) hem at the sides.

Making up lined curtains

1. Join the necessary widths of curtain fabric together with open seams. Leave the selvedges but slash diagonally at frequent intervals. Press the seams open. Join the linings in a similar way.

2. With the wrong side uppermost, spread the curtain on a flat surface, such as a large table or the floor, then turn 3-4 cm (1¼-1½ in) single widths down each long side of curtain. Herringbone into place.

3. Lay the curtain lining, wrong side downwards, over the curtain. Smooth down until quite flat. Turn back one-third (figure 12). Catch lining to curtain with a loop stitch every 10 cm (4 in) on most fabrics, 5 cm (2 in) on velvet curtains (figure 13). Turn back the third, turn in 1 cm (½ in) along this edge and place over curtain. Slip-stitch into position. Treat the other third in a similar way.

Note This linking holds the lining and curtain together.

4. Turn the top of the curtain over into position. Pin and tack. The depth of turn depends on the tape you are using.

5. Pin and tack the curtain tape in position, ready for machining. Stitch in place. Insert hooks.

6. Hang the curtains on curtain pulleys or track at this stage. Only in this way can you make sure that the interlinings and linings hang correctly.

7. Prepare the lower hems then mitre the corners. Slip-stitch each hem. The lower hems of curtain and lining are not stitched together (figure 14).

Weighting hems

The finished curtain hangs more evenly and with crisper folds if the lower hem is weighted. It is no longer necessary to cover and stitch in individual weights as a white plastic-covered weighting can now be purchased. It is sausage-like in appearance and available in three different weights: light-weight for use with sheer nets, medium-weight for medium-weight fabrics and a heavy quality for velvets, brocades, etc. Slip this weighting into the hem and anchor neatly in a recess at each end.

> Be sure to follow the maker's instructions carefully when using iron-on tape.
>
> Central heating has reduced the necessity for lined curtains.
>
> Take advantage of the modern designs, new light-weight fabrics and new widths now available.

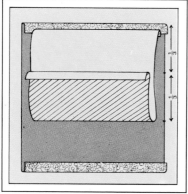

12 Attached lining, turn back a third

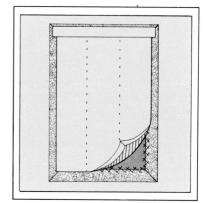

13 Attached lining, loop stitch

14 Stitched-in lining

Continental Quilts

This type of bed covering has become very popular over the last few years. Scandinavian in origin, continental quilts are not only very warm, but practical too. The quilt —or duvet—is covered with an easily removable slip. Together with a bottom sheet, these quilts cut bed-making to a minimum. A quick shake and you are ready to face the day. The simplicity of the duvet makes both its construction and its use quick and easy.

Sizes

It is of the greatest importance, because of the principle of this type of bed-cover, that the completed quilt should overhang both the bottom and sides of the bed. Allow an overhang of between 15-24 cm (6-9 in) generally, to ensure that the quilt will not slip off the bed when the occupant moves or turns over during sleep.

One of the major objections to these quilts in the early days was that they tended to make the bed look less attractive than one covered by the more traditional bed-clothes. This argument has now largely been overcome by the manufacture of attractively designed outer covers with matching sheets, pillow cases and a valance which fits over the base of the bed.

Note If planning to use a valance, make sure that the overhang of the quilt extends each side of the bed to just beyond the top of the base of the bed. An average double-sized bed will need a completed quilt measuring not less than 2 m (6½ ft) in length x 1·7 m (5½-6 ft) in width. A full-length single-bed quilt needs to measure approximately 2 m (6½ ft) x 1·25 m (4-4½ ft).

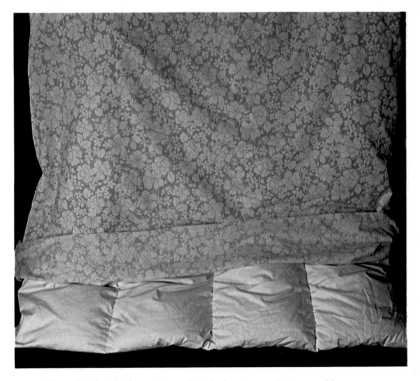

Four channels of a single continental quilt showing under removable cover

Fillings

One of the great advantages of continental quilts is their extreme lightness and warmth. These properties are due to the type and quality of filling used in the duvet. It is the insulation provided by the air trapped by the filling which provides the warmth rather than the quantity of filling used. So, to provide the necessary volume of filling which will entrap the required layer of air, it is important to use the best quality of filling possible.

Duck down or a proportion of this mixed with best-quality duck feather is used in commercially produced quilts. A 'down and feather' mixture contains more than 50 per cent of down, whereas a 'feather and down' mixture contains more than half its weight in feather. The greater the percentage of feather, the heavier becomes a given volume of filling, but the lower the price per unit weight of mixture. This variation of volume and weight means that a greater weight of the cheaper fillings must be used to give the same degree of insulation and warmth. So buy the best you can afford.

A cheaper alternative filling is Terylene or Dacron floss, so called because it resembles sugar-candy floss in appearance. This type of quilt is now very common and although it is not as warm as one filled with down, it is very suitable for use in summer, in a centrally heated room or in a situation where the quilt will need cleaning often— a child's room, for instance. It can also be used in colder rooms with extra bed-coverings.

Note The Terylene filling is not quite so easy to stuff into the channels of a quilt as down and feather filling.

Recycling Fillings from Old Quilts

Down filling is expensive, so if a good-quality, old quilt is available, it is economical to re-use it. This need not be a difficult or a messy operation. Unpick the stitching at one end of each pocket and then make an opening at one end of the quilt. Tack a pillow case or plastic bag *securely* over this opening and, working from the opposite end, slap the filling along the channels and out into the bag. Slap with the palm of the hand and so drive the filling along (figure 1). Alternatively, it is possible to insert a clean paper bag into some vacuum cleaners and then suck the filling out into the bag. Any vacuum cleaner used for this purpose must be completely free from dust.

Before using any reclaimed down or feather filling, examine it carefully. If it is composed largely of feathers with a large amount of quill, use it for cushions rather than a new quilt. Down and feather fillings go dead after a time—that is, they tend to lose resilience and become flat and heavy. If only a small proportion of the amount of filling required has been obtained from an old quilt, supplement it with a small quantity of new filling.

This will probably be more resilient and will have more volume than the older filling. Use it in the central channels of the new quilt for maximum warmth and comfort.

Quantities

The exact amount of filling required to fill a particular quilt will vary according to the quality of the filling, the temperature of the home in which it is to be used and the personal needs and the preferences of its future owner. A general guide is 1·5 kg ($3-3\frac{1}{2}$ lb) for a double quilt and 1 kg–1·2 kg ($2-2\frac{1}{2}$ lb) for a single quilt.

Cover Fabric

Select this to suit the type of filling being used. Use a down-proof fabric for a down or down/feather mixture. It is false economy to use a fabric which will allow this expensive filling to escape for, in addition to the mess, the quilt will gradually become less efficient. Down-proof cambric is a very finely woven fabric made of cotton which has been specially treated or 'proofed' to prevent the down escaping. So buy a good-quality cambric with all these features. The cambric is usually cream in colour, and 140–150 cm (56–60 in) wide. If one surface has a shiny glazed appearance, make up the cover so

that this surface is to the inside of the quilt on completion; this treated surface repels the down filling.

If using a Terylene filling, make the cover from a proofed Terylene or Polyester fabric or one which is a Terylene-Polyester mix. The quilt will then be completely washable, making it suitable for an invalid or child.

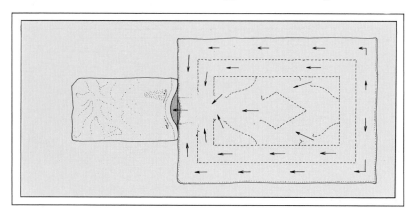

1 Emptying old quilt of down; it has been partially unpicked and the direction of the down is shown travelling into the collecting bag

in making up. Pin and tack in the seam allowances only and do not remove the tacking stitches. Set the machine to a very fine stitch and use a very fine needle; large needles leave equally large holes that form an easy escape route for the filling. Double-stitch the seams as a further preventive measure. Machine the first row of stitching 1 cm ($\frac{1}{2}$ in) from the edge of the fabric; the second row can be a row of straight stitches 2 mm ($\frac{1}{8}$ in) from edge or a row of zigzag stitches if a swing-needle machine is used. Once the stitching is complete, rub beeswax into the seams to fill any holes left by the needle.

Working Gussets in Quilts

The main difference, apart from size, between a continental quilt and the traditional 'eiderdown' quilt is that the new form of bed cover consists of channels formed by

A restful modern bedroom in which the style is set by the single bed with its matching continental quilt and tailored valance; not only is the quilt pleasant to look at and easy to sleep under once you are used to it, it also cuts out bed-making, for there are no blankets to shake and no fluff to gather under the bed. The continental quilt introduces a new way of sleeping

Basic Techniques for Making Quilt Covers

When using down as a filling together with specially treated fabric that prevents it escaping, be very careful not to destroy this property by mishandling the cover

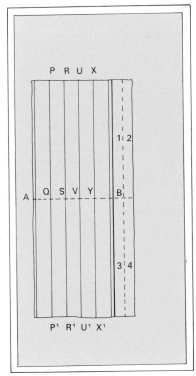

2 Cutting pattern for small single quilt 120 cm (48 in) wide

gussets. The top and bottom surface of the traditional quilt were machined together to form attractive 'quilted' designs. But this often meant that in some closely worked areas there was hardly any filling at all, so reducing the effectiveness of the quilt.

In continental quilts, however, the gussets—measuring 4–5 cm (1½–2 in) wide—run lengthways down the quilt, so ensuring that the filling is evenly distributed over the whole area of the cover. The channels also control the filling so that it cannot move around when in use. Yet another of the gussets' functions is to allow the underside of the quilt to move with the sleeper rather than being pulled off the bed. The under-surface moves freely while the upper surface remains static.

Quilt for Single Bed

Before buying the materials for the quilt, do check the size of your bed first to make sure you buy enough. For a bed measuring 91 x 185 cm (3 x 6 ft), the finished quilt should be 135 x 200 cm (4½ x 6½ ft). For this you will need approximately 4 m (4½ yd) high-quality down-proof cambric or Polyester, 140–150 cm (54–60 in) wide, 1–1·2 kg (2–2½ lb) filling and four or more reels of mercerized cotton (for down-proof fabric) or Polyester thread (figure 3, for other widths see figures 2, 4).

If your cover fabric is to be only 125 cm (48 in) wide, cut the gussets from closely woven tape measuring 8·5 m (9 yd) long by 4–5 cm (1½–2 in) wide.

Note The quantity of filling may have to be adjusted during the transition from imperial to metric as much is still sold in imperial packs. Any surplus may be used to make or supplement that in pillows.

Preparing the fabric

1. Working with the glazed surface of the fabric uppermost (i.e. with the wrong side facing you), mark off a strip measuring 127 cm (50 in) wide with chalk or pencil. This will give an overhang of 15 cm (6 in) and leave a strip of fabric 15 cm (6 in) wide for the gussets. Cut or tear along the marked line.

2. Cut or tear four strips 4–5 cm (1½–2 in) wide for the gussets from the narrower strip. These should measure 2 m (2¼ yd) in length.

Note If you require a wider overhang, use the whole width of the fabric for the bag and make gussets from tape or extra fabric. Tear this into strips and join as necessary.

3. Mark a seam allowance of 1 cm (½ in) along all four sides of the large rectangle with chalk or tacking.

4. Draw four pencil lines parallel to the long edges, so dividing the main piece of fabric for the cover into five equal channels, each measuring approximately 25 cm (10 in).

Note The narrower the channels,

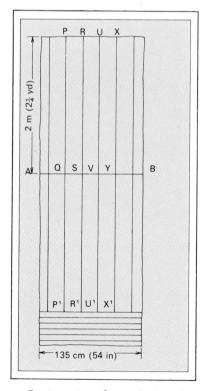

3 *Cutting pattern for standard single quilt 135 cm (54 in) wide*

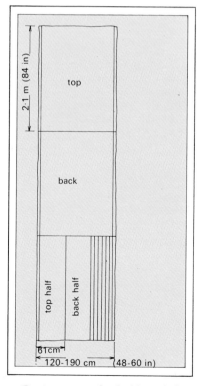

4 *Cutting pattern for double quilt from material of various widths*

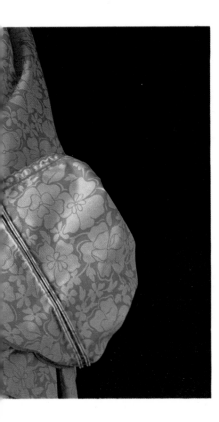

The parts that the casual eye does not usually reach: note the neatening effect of the scalloped edge

stitches within the 1-cm ($\frac{1}{2}$-in) seam allowance.

7. Using a fine needle and a very small stitch, machine down both long sides 1 cm ($\frac{1}{2}$ in) from the raw edges. Stitch down this edge a second time, keeping stitches just inside the raw edges or, if using a swing-needle on a machine, neatening the edges with zigzag stitches as you work.

8. Wax the rows of machining on both surfaces of the bag by rubbing into and along the seam allowances with a lump of beeswax.

Inserting the gusset

9. To shape the gussets, fold one end centrally and shape into a rounded point (figure 5). Shape the second end after the gusset has been inserted.

10. Turn the bag, wrong sides still outside, so that the open end is to your left.

11. Tuck the lower channel into the rest of the bag by folding along the line marked P-Q-P' (figure 6).

12. Place the pointed end of the gusset marked Q' to the right-hand end of the bag marked point Q, then tack one edge of the gusset to the folded edge marked Q-P. Check that the raw edge of the gusset is slightly higher than the fold of the bag. Work to within 8 cm (3 in) of the left-hand edge of the bag. Shape this end of the gusset as at the other end, so that it ends just over 1 cm ($\frac{1}{2}$ in) short of the edge of the bag. Stitch just inside the tacking stitches, which should be kept as close to the folded edge of the bag as possible. Working from the open end, tack the other side of the gusset to the fold marked Q-P. This enables the fold to be seen and the raw edge secured slightly higher than the fold itself. Work on a flat surface at all times. Stitch along this join to complete

the less filling they will hold, so 25 cm (10 in) is an ideal width.

5. Fold the fabric along the line marked A-B, the pencil lines on the outside.

6. Tack the two long sides of the bag together, keeping the tacking

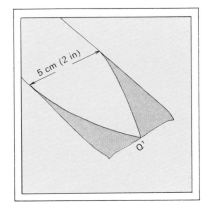

5 *Shaping the ends of the gussets inserted between channels*

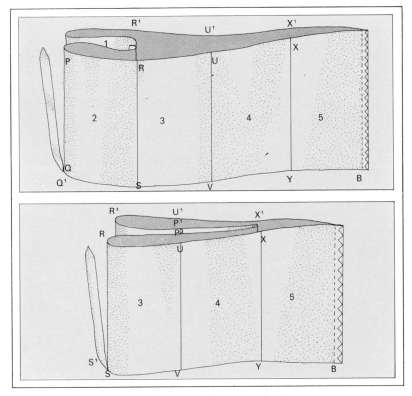

6 *(Top) Inserting the first gusset into a five-channel quilt*
7 *(Bottom) Inserting the second gusset into a continental quilt*

the insertion of the first gusset.
13. To insert the second gusset, tuck the completed channel together with the next section into the bag by folding along the second pencil line marked R-S-R′. The first gusset is now hidden and completed. Place the tip of the shaped second gusset to point S and attach as described before (figure 7).
14. Continue inserting the remaining two gussets completing each before moving on to the next. Once the last gusset has been completed, the whole of the quilt cover should be folded into the fifth channel so giving the appearance of a long thin sausage.
15. Push your arm down to the bottom of this tube, take hold of the edge of the bag and draw the compressed fabric forwards and the cover will open out (figure 8).

Filling the quilt

Each channel will require approximately 225 g (8 oz) of filling. If using Terylene or Dacron, insert this gradually, teasing each handful before use and then inserting to the bottom end of the channel. If using a down mixture, *securely* tack the end of the bag of filling to the end of the channel to avoid any escaping. Leave a small opening for inserting your hand. Then, gently ease the filling from the bag into the channel. When the filling of one channel is complete, roll the ends over and secure with paper clips.

Fill all the channels in this way. Then remove the paper clips and turn in the seam allowances along both edges. Tack together very close to the edge and secure with two rows of fine stitching 3 mm ($\frac{1}{8}$ in) apart. If the quilt still appears only partly filled, put it in a warm place so that the filling puffs up and gives the desired effect.

Quilt for Double Bed

The measurements will be 185 x 200 cm 6 x 6½ ft) for a double bed

measuring 135 x 190 cm (4½ x 6¼ ft).

To make a quilt this size, buy 6·5 m (7 yd) high-quality, down-proof cambric or Polyester, 140-150 cm (54-60 in) wide and 1·4-1·8 kg (3-4 lb) of filling (this is a general guide only).

Making up the quilt

1. Cut the fabric as shown in figure 4. It may be necessary to vary the sizes of the panels, but the aim is to produce two rectangles for the two sides of the cover, each measuring approximately 185 x 200 cm (6 x 6½ ft).
2. Stitch one part-width to the top section of the quilt, the other to the bottom section. Stitch all the seams and wax in the usual way.
3. Prepare the gussets from the spare fabric or tape as described for the single quilt.
4. Mark the positions for the gussets on the wrong sides of the two quilt sections. Seven channels will give a satisfactory result but if less filling is to be used, divide the quilt into eight channels.
5. Place the two halves of the quilt together, right sides together, with the pencil lines visible. Tack these together, keeping the stitches in the seam allowance. Leave one short end open. Double-machine around the two long and one short edges.
6. Insert the gussets, fill and close the fourth side as for a single quilt.

Outer Covers and Valances

Manufacturers take considerable trouble to produce attractive co-ordinated ranges of plain and patterned sheeting for making up into covers, valances, sheets and pillow cases. So the argument that quilts do not make for an attractive bedroom has been largely invalidated by fashion and public demand.

It is important to choose fabrics which are light in weight and require little or no ironing. The

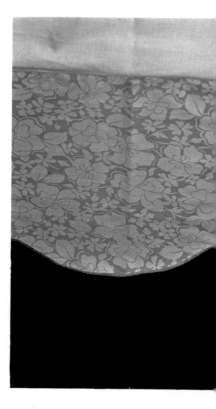

Polyester-and-cotton-mix fabrics are ideal for the purpose. You will find making up both outer cover and valance much easier if a very wide material can be found which requires little or no joining. Such fabrics are now widely available.

When cutting the outer cover, make it 5-8 cm (2-3 in) larger than the quilt itself so that the quilt is in no way restricted. This would

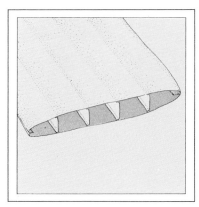

8 Cross-section of quilt showing gussets inserted

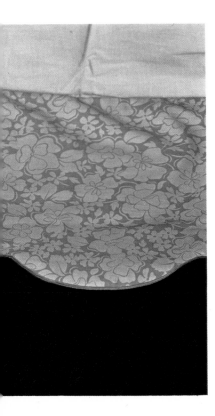

alternative method is to have a side opening closed by several tapes or invisible fasteners.

If you find it impossible to find a wide enough Polyester cotton fabric, buy sheets and make up a cover with these. There should be enough spare fabric left over to make matching pillow cases. There is plenty of scope for economy here, which is preferable to economizing on the quilt itself.

Making up a Valance

A valance fits over the base of the bed, under the mattress. If it is to retain a trim and tailored appearance it should fit accurately. The frill, which falls from the edge of the base to within 2·5 cm (1 in) of the floor may be gathered, pleated or tailored (plain at the sides with an inverted pleat at each of the bottom corners). This design is very popular at the moment and is much more economical of fabric.

Cutting out the valance

Allow 1 cm (½ in) seam allowance along the top edge and 5 cm (2 in) for a hem (figure 9).

1. Cut one piece of fabric to the size of the top of the base, plus 1 cm (½ in) seam allowances all round. This can be of a different cheaper fabric but should be of a man-made fibre for quick drying.

2. Cut the frill as follows, basing your measurements on the combined length of the two long sides plus one width of the bed.

Notes For spaced pleats allow twice the above length; for a gathered frill allow one and a half to two times the above length depending on the texture of the fabric and your financial resources; for a tailored frill, allow the length of the two sides plus the width of the bed plus an allowance of 50–60 cm (16-24 in) for the two inverted pleats at the corners.

3. Cut four strips for the mitred border; there should be two the

length of the bed plus 2·5 cm (1 in) and two the width of the bed plus 2·5 cm (1 in)—all 10 cm (4 in) wide.

Making up the valance

1. Join the four border strips together, mitring the corners neatly so that the whole fits on the large rectangle exactly.

2. Prepare the frill, neatening the two ends with a narrow hem.

3. With the wrong sides facing, tack the frill to the base. When making a pleated frill, arrange so that a pleat ends at each corner. Even with spaced pleats there will be an inverted pleat at the two bottom corners. Arrange and distribute gathers evenly, with a little extra fullness at each corner.

4. Fit the mitred border to the valance with the right side of the border to the right side of the frill, then tack and stitch 1 cm (½ in) from the raw edges.

5. Turn the border on to the base, turn in 1 cm (½ in) along the raw edge and stitch the folded edge down on to the base.

6. Fit the valance on to the base of the bed and turn up the lower hem so that it clears the floor by approximately 2·5 cm (1 in).

Laundering

Having chosen fabrics for the outer cover and valance that require the minimum of maintenance, never allow them to become too soiled, and wash with care. Use water that is hand-hot and do not allow the fabrics to soak for long periods. Rinse well and then spin very lightly. Too hot water, long soaking and over-spinning can result in permanent creasing.

(Top centre) The scalloped edge of the tailored valance attached to its plain base cover; the valance and its matching continental quilt are made in an attractive patterned cotton polyester fabric that can easily be laundered

reduce its effectiveness. Ensure that the outer cover can be easily removed for laundering. The neatest design is one incorporating what is called 'the housewife flap', the flap being at the top edge and, unlike that on a pillow, situated on the outside of the cover. You can decorate the edge of the flap with a suitable trimming or decorative machine-stitching as desired. An

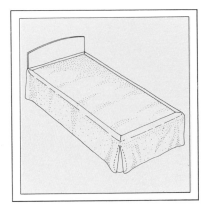

9 *A valance fitted on to a standard single bed, inverted pleats at corner*

Cushions, curtains and quilts materials suppliers

Berks.	Caleys High St WINDSOR
	Heelas Broad St READING
Cambs.	Robert Sayle St Andrews St CAMBRIDGE
Hants.	Knight and Lee Palmerston Rd SOUTHSEA
Lancs.	George Henry Lee Basnett St LIVERPOOL
	Russell Trading Co. 75 Paradise St LIVERPOOL (fabrics and stuffing)
London	John Barnes Finchley Rd NW3
	Distinctive Trimmings 17D Kensington Church St W8
	Distinctive Trimmings 11 Marylebone Lane W1
	Jones Brothers Holloway Rd N7
	Peter Jones Sloane Square SW1
	John Lewis Brent Cross Shopping Centre NW11
	John Lewis Oxford St W1
	Pratts Streatham High Rd SW16
	Russell and Chapple 23 Monmouth St WC2 (canvas and hessians)
	Trewin Brothers Queen's Rd WATFORD
Northumb.	Bainbridge Eldon Sq NEWCASTLE-UPON-TYNE
Notts.	Jessop and Son Victoria Centre NOTTINGHAM
Wilts.	Mace and Nairn 89 Crane St SALISBURY (special threads)
Yorks.	Cole Brothers Barkers Pool SHEFFIELD
Scotland Lothian	John Lewis St James Centre EDINBURGH

Cushions, curtains & quilts materials suppliers

Specialists	
Fabrics and stuffing	Russell Trading Co. 75 Paradise St LIVERPOOL
Trimmings	Distinctive Trimmings Co. Ltd. 17D Kensington Church St LONDON W8
	Distinctive Trimmings Co. Ltd. 11 Marylebone Lane LONDON W1
Specialist threads	Mace & Nairn 89 Crane St SALISBURY Wilts
Natural hessians, twills, duck, canvas	Russell & Chapple 23 Monmouth St LONDON WC2

Books for further reference

Curtain Making, Joanne Prior, NFWI, 1967
Streamlined Curtains and Covers, Renee and Julian Robinson, Bodley Head, 1968
Perfect Way to Make Exciting Curtains, Rufflette Style Book
Window Curtaining, Bess Yiemont, US Government Press, 1930

Light and shade...

To achieve your 'impossible dream' of a lampshade, you may have to make it yourself. The following pages show you how to do it. Whether you want to read comfortably in a good light or relax at your ease in restful shade, the choice can be yours. Shades can be firm or soft, bowed or fluted, to suit whatever ambience you wish to create. As highlights add beauty to a woman's face, so can shades impart discretion to her home.

Making Lamp-shades

Making lampshades is a craft that has increased in popularity over the last few years. There are numerous reasons for this:

(a) It is an area of soft furnishing and the wider art of interior design that has caught the imagination of the general public.

(b) A homemade lampshade is very economical to make. You will realize this when you browse around your local department store and see the high cost of commercially produced shades. In all craftwork it is the labour involved which makes the finished article expensive and, as a homemade shade requires very little equipment and only small amounts of fabric, it makes good sense to 'do-it-yourself'. Browsing round the department store will also enable you to keep abreast of modern styles and trends.

(c) Even a first attempt can result in a very attractive piece of work. All you need to do is to make careful and adequate preparations and be very patient when fitting the covers to the frame.

(d) With some basic knowledge, you can make a shade that is perfect in shape, colour and design for a particular room. Made from small pieces of fabric left from large items of home furnishings, such as curtains, cushions or bed covers, the shades can help to tie up the colour scheme in a room.

(e) By using your initiative in combining different fabrics and the ways in which you use the fabrics, you will be able to make completely

Unpainted frames showing bowed empire types with gimbal fitting (back) and pendant types (front)

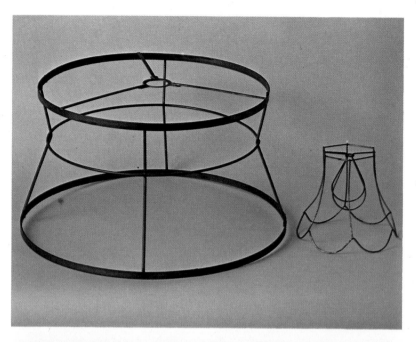

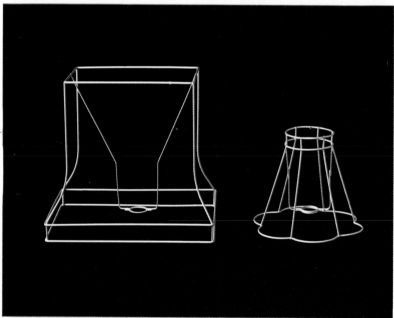

and possibly with even greater frequency. This is probably because lampshades are quicker and cheaper to replace than curtains and chair covers – even cushions!

Buying the Frame

The success of any shade depends on how it relates to the base of the lamp and how it fits into its surroundings. It is therefore important to buy the correct type, style and size of frame. The type of frame relates to its style of fitting, and this depends on whether the shade is to be hung from the ceiling, fitted on to a standard-size base, a reading lamp or a candle-style fitting.

The large majority of frames consist of two rings, one of which incorporates some type of fitting to hold it in position. If the frame is to be covered with a soft fabric, the two main rings will be held apart by a number of struts. If a firm material is to form the cover, the two rings are all that is needed.

When buying a frame for a standard shade, choose one that is made of stout wire, otherwise the frame, which is put under strain in the making, will lose its shape. In this type of frame there is also a third ring suspended from the top ring by three struts. This ensures that when the shade is in position the bulb is half way between the rings at the top and bottom.

You will need a 'pendant' fitting for a shade to be hung from the ceiling. This has a small ring which fits on to the adaptor and is joined to the top ring by two bars. Some rings used with firm materials have a recessed pendant, the small ring being held about 2 cm (1 in) below the level of the top ring.

If you want a frame for a reading lamp, select one with a 'gimbal' fitting where the small ring is held near the lower ring by two long arms attached to the top ring. These arms are usually hinged, so that you can tilt the shade to redirect the light as required.

original unique lampshades.

(f) The craft has something to offer everyone, irrespective of experience and talent, how much money they have to spend or how much time they can devote to the craft.

(g) You can make a lampshade in no time at all. A firm shade, for example, can be completed in only one evening.

(Top) Tripod fitting and butterfly clip
(Bottom) Square and fluted frames

Lampshades and Fashion

The style of lampshades changes with the times, just as it does in other branches of soft furnishings,

It is very important to get a good balance between the lamp base and frame. If at all possible, take the base to the shop when buying a frame. There is no infallible rule governing the proportions, as these are most affected by the style itself. If you do make a mistake in selection, shops are often willing to change a frame providing it has not been damaged in any way.

If you want to make shades for wall lights or a candle-style lamp that hangs from the ceiling, there are two styles of suitable fitting. The basic rules are that if the bulb hangs downwards, you need a frame with a standard 'pendant' fitting, but if the bulb faces upwards, the frame needs to incorporate a 'butterfly-clip' type of fitting.

Frame and Bulb

Any shade—other than one made of china or glass—will scorch or burn if you use too strong a bulb for the size of shade. There should be plenty of room between the bulb and shade so that air can circulate freely. Do not use a bulb stronger than 60 watts under a candle-shade and take care when using frames with a gimbal fitting that the shade is not tilted to such a degree that the cover touches the bulb. If this happens, the shade will certainly become scorched or singed.

Examine any frame carefully before purchase. You will have

Butterfly clips adapt these shades for wall lights or candle-style lamps

problems if the joints of fitting-to-ring and struts-to-rings come apart when the shade is being covered or used. The struts should finish level with the rings and should not protrude at all to give sharp projections that will cut through any fabric and will mean a waste of your time, energy and money.

Choosing the Right Style

It is in the style or shape of the frame that the effect of fashion is seen. The bowed-empire-style lampshade has always been a great favourite. This type of frame sometimes has a collar at the top or the bottom. The drum, either round or oval, is another favourite and is a particularly suitable frame for all forms of pleating. Another basic style which survives in a variety of forms is the 'Tiffany' shade, and this is one that even a complete beginner can attempt with confidence.

Equipment

One of the most attractive features of lampshade-making is that it is not necessary to buy a vast amount of expensive equipment. Indeed, if you practise craftwork to any degree, you will find that you probably already possess nearly everything you need.

You must have two pairs of scissors – a large pair, with blades measuring 15-20 cm (6-8 in), for cutting fabrics, and a smaller pair for really fine work. These should have fine points for trimming raw edges. If you plan to use any of the firmer materials available, such as fibreglass, it is an advantage to use an old pair of dressmaking or kitchen scissors in order to avoid ruining your better pair.

It is useful to have a selection of needles, but you will certainly need a short, stout needle for stitching the fabric to the frame. This will have to be replaced fairly frequently as

the tip hits the metal frame repeatedly during stitching. A blunt needle will only pull the threads and disfigure the fabric and shade.

You will use a lot of pins when making soft shades. The smallest of these – called 'Lillikins' – are ideal for this type of work. The longer the pin, the more likely it is to scratch you, thus leading to the fabric being soiled with blood. The small, sharp 'Lillikins' pass easily through the very tight binding and are also less likely to leave holes in the fabric.

Working with a large number of pins can be painful, and they do get pulled out very easily. So it is useful to have a piece of plastic foam over your knee – it acts as protection and doubles as a pincushion.

If using a firm material for your shade, use spring-type clothes pegs instead of pins when holding the material to the rings. If the cover is to be thonged to the rings, use a leather punch to form the holes.

Preparing the Frame

This is probably the most important stage in the making of any shade. The method of preparation varies, depending on the type of shade and the cover fabric you are using. The joints of the metal should be smooth – if they are not, file them carefully.

Some frames can be bought

already prepared, with a coating of enamel or plastic. These are excellent but much more expensive than the untreated frames. To save money, buy an unprepared frame and paint it. This prevents it rusting and is particularly important if the frame is intended for use in a damp atmosphere or if it will require washing. Paint the complete frame, including the fitting, as any exposed metal will eventually darken. Use a fast-drying enamel or cellulose paint at least 48 hours before the frame is to be used. If you do not intend to bind the struts, but are using an external lining, paint the struts the same colour as the lining (e.g. on a Tiffany-style shade). With gimbal frames, do not allow the hinge to become set.

Binding the Frame

There was a time when both rings and all the struts of all shades were bound, irrespective of how the cover was to be made and attached. This has now been found to be unnecessary and even detrimental in some cases. Any part of the frame to which fabric is to be stitched must be bound, but struts which will not have fabric attached to them can be left unbound. If you do bind them, the ridges of the binding will slowly become visible through the cover, and will collect dirt, so spoiling the appearance of

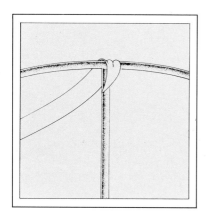 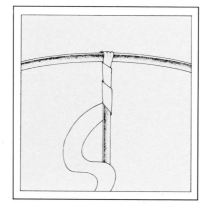 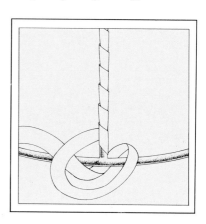

1 *Commence binding with tapered point*   2 *Binding at acute angle*   3 *Looping of binding at bottom of ring*

the work. Better to avoid regret.

Binding is the most important part of making a fabric shade because, if the binding slips, you will find it impossible to get a taut cover. As you progress, check that you cannot move the binding. If you can do so, you must undo it and start again.

Materials suitable for binding rings

Balloon-lined shades in which the struts are hidden—use 10-mm ($\frac{3}{8}$-in) cotton tape.

Unlined shades in which the rings are to be covered, for example, by trimming—use 10-mm ($\frac{3}{8}$-in) tape.

Unlined shade, when the rings are visible—use 10-mm ($\frac{3}{8}$-in) tape, overbound with strips of cover fabric, or ribbon or Paris binding to match the cover.

Materials for binding struts (if necessary)

Balloon-lined shade—where the struts are hidden—use 10-mm ($\frac{3}{8}$-in) tape.

External lining or unlined shade—use selvedge from lining 1 cm ($\frac{1}{2}$ in) wide, or strips of lining fabric 15 mm ($\frac{5}{8}$ in) wide with one raw edge turned in by ironing, or matching ribbon or Paris binding.
Note When choosing tape, select

one of soft cotton (not linen or any heavily dressed fabric, as these will leave a puckered surface when moulded to the metal).

Binding a Frame

Begin by binding any struts which are to remain bound; then bind the rings. If the struts are to be bound only to allow for fitting of the cover or lining of a shade (as with a tailored cover or lining), bind the rings first. The struts are then bound for the fitting, and this tape is removed before the cover is attached.

Binding a strut

1. Cut a length of tape or other binding 1$\frac{1}{2}$ times the length of the strut, and taper one end. Place the tapered end over the top ring where the strut joins the ring (figure 1).
2. Bring the long end of the tape round and bind in the tapered end. Keep the binding tape at a very acute angle to the strut, binding so that there is a minimum of overlap (figure 2). The greater the overlap, the more bulky the finished binding; the aim is to achieve the smoothest binding possible. Continue until you reach the bottom ring.
3. Loop the end of the tape around the ring to form a knot and pull the tape tightly (figure 3). Trim off the

excess tape to 3 mm ($\frac{1}{8}$ in) from ring.

Binding the rings

4. Cut a length of binding equal to twice the circumference of the ring. Taper the end of the binding and place this end under the ring at the top left of a strut. Turn the tapered end to the right and commence binding in this direction (figure 4). Keep the tape at a very acute angle as before and bind to the next strut (figure 5).
5. Work one extra wrap and then take the tape over the top of the strut and bind the next section of the ring (figure 6). This extra twist just before the strut enables you to start binding the second section at an acute angle and so avoids any bulk which would result if a 'figure of eight' was worked at the top of each strut. Continue binding around the ring until it is completely bound. Fasten the end of the binding to the beginning of the ring binding with a few 'Streatley' stitches (figure 7). Trim away any excess tape (note that the raw edges are not turned in, as this would produce too much bulk). The join and the stitching must be on the outside of the frame so that they are hidden by the cover even if the frame is unlined. Bind the lower ring in the same way.

(Over) Drum shades may be made from firm or soft material

4 *Commence binding at top of strut*

5 *Extra twist at top of strut*

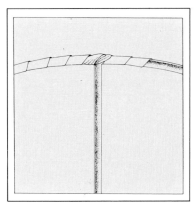

6 *Commence new section at acute angle*

Binding for a firm shade

As there are no struts in this case you will need to modify the previous instructions. For a ring with an attached fitting, begin the binding over the junction of the ring and fitting. Plain rings have no such aid, and if you start the binding by just folding the tape over the metal, it will spin round. To avoid this, place the end of the tape over the ring at an angle and secure in position with a dab of a clear adhesive. Allow this to dry. The ring will then be easy to bind. Finish off as for the strutted frame.

Stitches

Most of the work on a lampshade requires hand stitching. Streatley stitch—already mentioned—is very useful. It is strong, neat and allows you to cut the fabric right back to the stitching without fear of fraying.

To work Streatley stitch insert the needle into the tape or fabric, so that it is at right angles to the ring, and draw the thread through. Pick up the same piece of fabric a second time, then take the needle forward for 3 mm ($\frac{1}{8}$ in) and repeat the double-stitch (figure 7).

For stitching firm material to a ring, use Streatley stitch or a running stitch. Hold the top edge of the material level with the top of the ring and pass the stitches into the binding at the bottom of the ring (figure 8).

When stitching a trimming to a finished shade, work invisible stitches. A form of herringbone is best for this. Insert the needle behind the point where it emerges and repeat, so that when the thread is tightened, the tiny stitch sinks into the edging (figure 9).

You can join side seams on tailored shades most satisfactorily by machine stitching. Set the machine for a small stitch and check that the tension is not too tight. If it is, cracks may appear when the cover or lining is fitted and tightened on to the frame.

Materials

The materials used for making lampshades fall into two categories: firm materials and soft woven fabrics.

Firm Materials

The range of finishes on firm fabrics is extensive: there are woven fabrics bonded on to a rigid backing, fabrics with straw-like finishes or alternatively you can buy a plain backing with a self-adhesive surface, on which to place your own fabric. Pulled linen panels are sometimes mounted on to a stiff backing but remember that cardboard-backed shades cannot be washed.

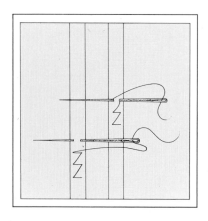

7 Streatley stitch

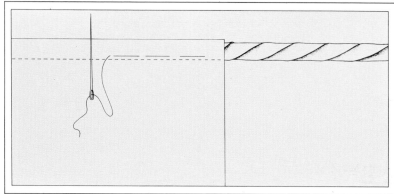

8 Optional stitch for firm shades, stab stitch passes through binding

Fibreglass provides a range of attractively designed materials and has the advantage that it can be washed. Firm shades fit particularly well into modern furnishing schemes.

Soft Fabrics

There is a tremendous range of these to choose from, and both dress and furnishing weight are suitable. The following points are worthy of consideration when making your choice:

(a) The amount of light you require to be transmitted through your lampshade. Dark colours absorb light and should be used only on television lights, etc.

(b) Relate the size of the frame to any pattern on the fabric. This is especially important when using furnishing fabrics. Large patterns might be suitable on a standard shade but would be most unsuitable for a small wall light.

(c) Decide what type of cover you want. Swathing, ruching and the various forms of pleating require really light sheer fabrics, such as chiffon.

(d) Do not forget the effect of light under the fabric—some brocades completely lose their pattern when subjected to a light bulb.

(e) Consider the texture of the fabric in relation to the type of frame. Very stiff fabrics cannot be used to make a tailored cover for a deeply bowed shade, for example. The fabric would have to be attached panel by panel. On bowed drums you will have to fit the outer-cover on the cross, so, though a striped fabric, for example, would not be suitable, one with a check could be used if the checks were carefully balanced at the seams.

Linings

Linings are not difficult to make or insert and they greatly improve the appearance and effectiveness of a shade. They fulfil a variety of uses:

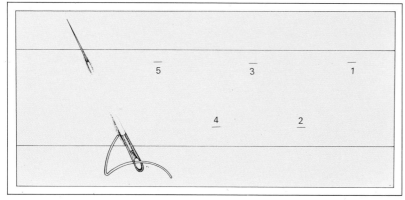

9 Stitch used for attaching braid: a form of herringbone stitch

(a) Balloon linings—which are fitted inside the frame—hide the struts. This is an advantage in hanging shades.

(b) They give extra body to the cover if the fabric being used is especially light or delicate—chiffon, for example. An external lining (which is fitted outside the frame) is essential with lace.

(c) They can affect the colour of transmitted light—a pink or peach lining will give a soft, warm light; a deep crimson gives a dramatic rosy glow.

(d) They can increase the amount of reflected light—a white lining under a dark cover will always improve the quality of the light.

Types of lining

You can fit a lining outside the struts—this is called an 'external' lining and is used under open fabrics such as lace or drawn- or pulled-thread work. This type of lining is also suitable for candle shades, where an internal or balloon lining might scorch or burn. You can make it as a tailored cover or in separate panels. Use it also on frames such as the Tiffany style where it is impossible to line the shade internally.

The lining can be made to fit inside the frame. This is an 'internal' or balloon lining. It may usually be cut on the cross or the straight but

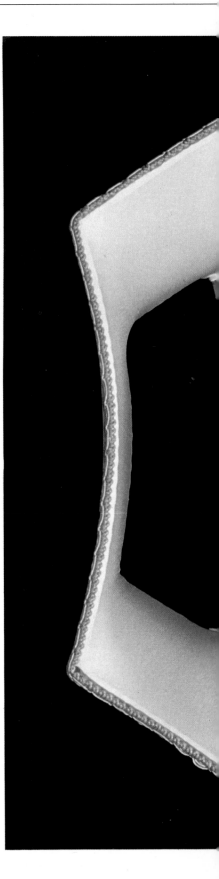

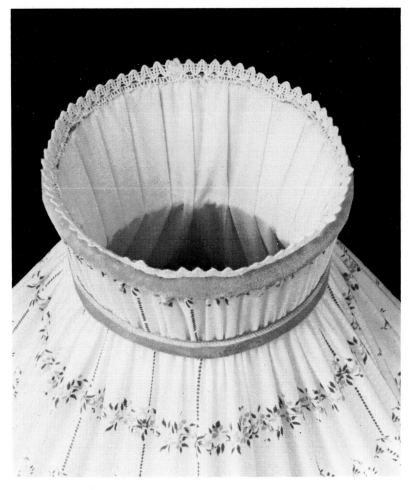

(Above) The necessary fullness of the lining has been neatly pleated
(Right) Lining on the right is external, but on the left, internal

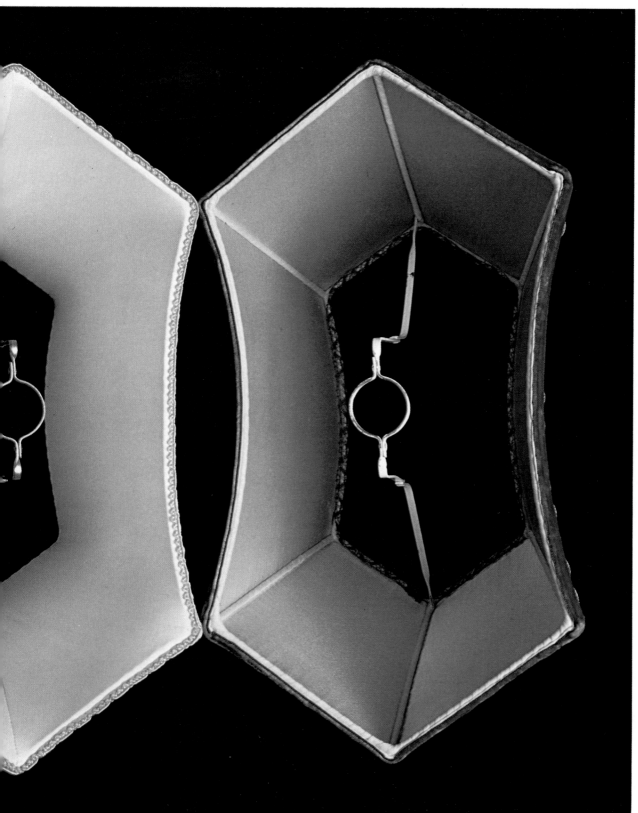

there are exceptions. When working on a drum frame, for example, the lining must be on the straight of the fabric.

A pleated or gathered lining can be made for use inside drum or empire shades which have straight struts.

The texture and colour of the cover may demand an internal and external lining. Only you can decide whether this is necessary or not.

Cutting a Tailored Cover or Lining

Covers and linings for some styles—a bowed empire shade, for example—can be cut either on the straight or the cross of the fabric, but if a cover for a drum frame is cut on the cross, the fabric will pull in across the middle of the frame, thus distorting the drum. For this reason, work the fabric for a straight-sided drum on the straight of the thread.

A cover for a bowed drum, on the other hand, must be cut on the cross. If you cut this cover on the straight of the fabric and make it up as a tailored cover, you will find it impossible to get the waisted middle point of the cover over the larger top or bottom rings. When it is cut on the cross, however, the central area will stretch and there will be no such problem.

A tailored cover is defined as one which is made up into one piece. This usually means constructing a 'tube' which is then fixed to the frame. It is not necessary to neaten the seams when joining the various sections of the cover. Most tailored shades consist of two pieces of fabric but some are made of four or even more. In a Tiffany frame, for example, the texture and amount of 'give' in the fabric determines how many sections need to be cut.

An alternative to a tailored shade, when using soft fabrics, is to make

Bowed drum shade with tailored cover cut on the cross; lining cut on straight

up and attach individual panels separately. This method makes it possible to use any fabric on the straight of the grain, to fit any type of frame. When attaching fabric in this way, neaten the outside of the cover along the struts to which the panels have been sewn, to cover all the raw edges. You could use braid, crossway strips, etc., for this purpose.

It is unwise to make shades using firm materials in separate sections. The trimming on the struts would be far too fussy for today's fashions.

When fitting a balloon lining, you can choose between cutting it on the cross or straight, but consider how closely the lining will hang to the frame after it has been inserted. Linings cut on the cross tend to bow away from the struts, and therefore hang closer to the bulb. This effect is not at all desirable in small shades but can be very pleasing on larger shades, especially those for standard lamp-bases.

Linings cut on the straight of the fabric must be fitted and assembled very accurately. There is no margin here at all for adjustment during fitting as there is when using a cover cut on the cross.

Methods of Fitting Tailored Covers and Linings

Linings and covers should both be fitted to the outside of the frame, with the wrong side of the fabric facing you.

If you are making the cover or lining in two sections, bind a pair of opposite struts. For example, if there are six struts on the frame, bind those numbered 1 and 4; if there are eight struts, bind 1 and 5. You then fit the cover over half the frame.

There are two ways of fitting a tailored cover and lining—with the fabric on the cross, and with the fabric on the straight.

The fabric on the cross

1. Lay the frame on its side.

2. Place the fabric, wrong side uppermost, and on the true cross, so that it covers half the frame. The point will fall over the top of the frame with some fullness.

3. Insert temporary pins at the top and bottom of the two bound struts at points marked A, B, C and D (figure 10).

4. Insert a pin every 1 cm ($\frac{1}{2}$ in) along the strut from A to B.

5. Return to the top of the strut, point A, and follow the grain or thread of the fabric until it reaches either the lower ring or the strut marked D-C, depending on the height of the frame (figures 10 and 11). This is point X.

6. Tighten along the line A-X and pin.

7. Continue pinning from X to B, tightening the fabric against the pins inserted between A-B and along the grain of the fabric. Any puckers that develop will disappear later.

8. Insert a pin at the top of both the intervening struts, points P and Q.

9. Begin pinning along the strut from C to D, inserting pins every 1 cm ($\frac{1}{2}$ in) and tightening against the bottom ring. If the shade is to be shaped as in figure 10, complete the pinning from X to D.

10. Mark the fabric very lightly with a pencil along the line of the pins on the two side struts and along the top ring. Do *not* mark along the bottom ring. Cut away any surplus fabric that extends to 2·5 cm (1 in) below the bottom ring but leave the triangle of fabric at the top of the frame.

11. Remove the pins and lift the half cover from the frame. Place this marked pattern on the remaining half of the fabric, right sides facing, with the pencil marks uppermost. The grain of the two pieces must match.

12. Pin down the lines of the struts on the pencil marks and then tack just outside the pins. Tailor tack

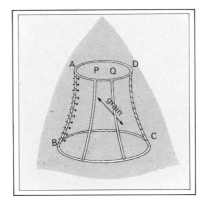

10 Fitting cover, squat frame

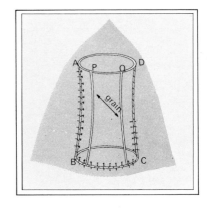

11 Fitting cover, tall frame

along the pencil line, marking the position of the top ring.

13. Machine along the line of the struts, beginning 2·5 cm (1 in) before the line of the top ring and continue the same distance below the end of the pencilled lines (figure 12).

14. Trim the seams to 3 mm ($\frac{1}{8}$ in). Oversew by hand or overlock with zigzag stitching if the fabric is liable to fray. Do not work a second row of straight stitching as this restricts the amount of 'give' in the seam during fitting.

The fabric on the straight

1. Place the frame on its side.

2. Lay the fabric over the frame with the straight of the grain running from the centre of the top ring to the centre of the bottom ring. Tighten the fabric from side to side across the centre of the frame, then insert a pin at the midpoint of the strut marked A–B at point P. Tighten from P and insert a pin at Q in the middle of C–D (figure 13).

3. Put in temporary pins at X and Y but do *not* tighten the fabric between these two points.

4. Return to pinning the side struts. Work upwards and downwards from P and Q until the fabric is pinned to the entire length of the struts.

Note Horizontal puckers will appear as the pinning progresses but these will disappear when you pin the fabric to the two rings.

5. Pin the fabric to the top and bottom rings, stretching it just enough to remove the puckers. If you pull too tightly vertically, the shape will be lost—a very common fault with covers fitted on the straight, of the material.

6. Trim the fabric to within 2·5 cm (1 in) of each side strut and to within 5 cm (2 in) of the top and bottom rings.

7. Mark and remove from the frame.

8. Place the half lining over the remaining fabric, matching the grain of the two pieces.

9. Pin along the side strut lines. As this lining is cut on the straight of the fabric and fitted on the outside of the frame, it may be necessary to reduce it slightly before inserting it into the shade. Draw a second line just inside the original lines—3 mm ($\frac{1}{8}$ in) inside at the same level of the rings and bowing it in 1 cm ($\frac{1}{2}$ in) at the centre of the seam (figure 14).

10. Tack the seams with small stitches and test the lining carefully inside the frame. If there is still fullness, increase the seam allowances; if too tight, release one or both. Only a little adjustment will be necessary.

Detail of bowed drum shade on previous page: here you can clearly see the grain running diagonally across the fabric. Antique lace appliquéd before lining

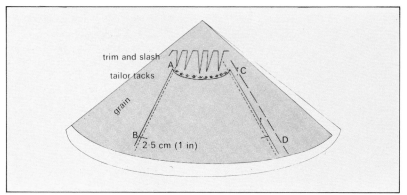

12 *Assembling cover on cross of fabric, two halves on matching grain*

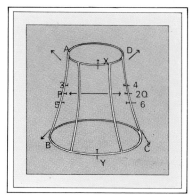

13 *Method of fitting on straight*

Fitting Lace for Covers

Lace is fitted on the straight of the fabric to gain the maximum amount of stretch. If the lace is so stiff that it will not bed to the frame, wash it before use. It is not practical to mark lace with a pencil, so outline the pattern of the half cover with a coloured tacking thread. Do not tack into the binding.

Note For all lampshade covers, whichever method of fitting you are using, the fabric should lie close to the frame and touch all the struts before it is marked. It should be completely free of wrinkles, bubbles and puckering.

Fitting an Internal Lining

On plain tailored shades, it is usual to insert the internal lining before attaching the cover. If the cover is made of a very strong material or velvet, fit and stitch the cover to the frame before attaching the lining. Also fit pleated, ruched and swathed covers before inserting the lining. In each of these cases, the tightening of the covers could cause a lining already inserted to become slack.

1. Slash the lining to within 4 cm (1½ in) of the tailor tacks marking the line of the top ring. Cut the tacks so the lining can be opened out.

2. Remove the binding from the two temporarily bound struts.

3. Place the lining inside the frame and pin the lining to the tops of the struts along the tacked line. Check that the seams fall over two of the struts. The lining will need slashing more deeply where the fittings meet the rings.

4. Turn the shade upside down and pin the seams to the bottom of the two struts tightening against the top ring.

5. Working on both sides of first one seam and then the other, pin the fabric to the lower ring, using both hands to keep the seam lines

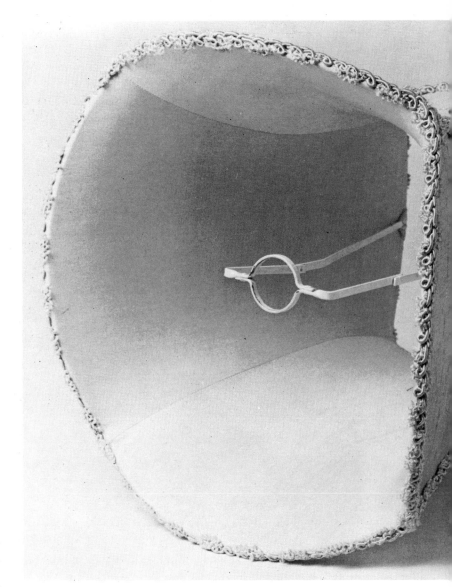

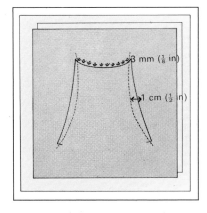

14 *Assembling lining on straight*

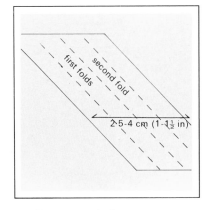

15 *Crossway strip for neatener*

3 mm (⅛ in)

1 cm (½ in)

first folds

second fold

2·5–4 cm (1–1½ in)

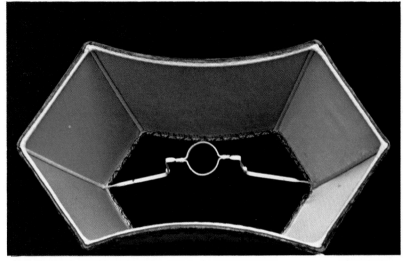

*Internal lining in four sections joined
by single seams
(Right) External lining*

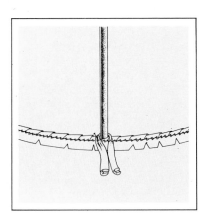

16 Neatener in position

running down the line of the strut.
If wrinkles appear, remove them by
tightening the fabric at right angles
to the wrinkles. You will find that
the lining needs tightening in alternate directions two or three times.
6. Stitch the lining to the frame with
Streatley stitch, making sure that
the stitches are on the outside of the
rings (these stitches will then be
hidden by the cover). Trim away
any surplus fabric. Then examine
carefully for any stray threads and
remove them, otherwise they will
be visible through the cover when
the lamp is lit.

Neatening the top ring

When fitting the lining inside the
frame, the lining fabric has been
slashed where the fitting bars join
the ring. These raw edges have to
be neatened. However careful you
are, you will find it advisable to
cover them up some way.
  Make these 'neateners' by cutting
crossway strips of the lining fabric
2·5-4 cm (1-1½ in) wide (figure 15).
Turn in the raw edges to meet
in the centre of the strip and then
fold in two. Fit this rouleau around
the junction of the fitting and the
ring. Lay the two ends side by side,
and then stitch them to the outside
of the ring, trimming the surplus
away (figure 16).

Fitting the cover

7. Place the cover over the frame,
matching the seams of the cover to
those of the lining and fit in exactly
the same way as the lining. When
the fitting is completed, the cover
should sit on the frame touching all
the struts and be free of any fullness.
8. Stitch the cover in position, but
work the stitches along the bottom
of the ring this time.
9. Roll the surplus fabric back on to
the cover. None of the stitches
securing the lining should be visible.
Secure the turning with a row of
single diagonal stitches (figure 17)
a distance of 3 mm (⅛ in) above the
edge of the fold. Trim away any
surplus fabric.

Tailored Shade, Tiffany-style

Tiffany shades are enjoying a revival
in popularity. The name comes
from the designer of the late nine-
teenth and early twentieth century
who worked in stained glass to
create multi-coloured lamps that
are now collectors' items. Many are
fringed—either with beads, to give
an exotic effect, or to add a touch
of luxury to a basically simple style.
1. Paint the frame to match the
lining (if used) or the underside of
the cover fabric. Bind the top and
bottom rings, and the struts to

113

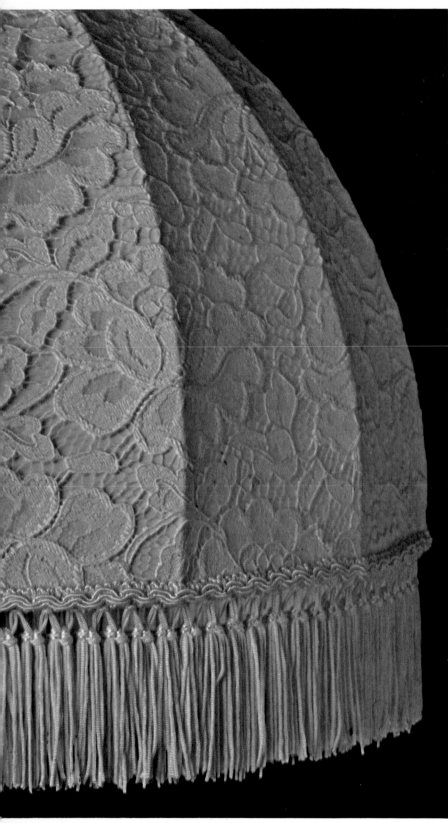

which the material is to be stitched. All struts may be bound if desired, the binding matching, in colour, the lining or underside of the cover.

2. Place the fabric over a quarter or half of the frame depending on the 'give' in the fabric. A stiffer material will have to be worked in four quarter panels. Fit the sections on the true cross. Insert pins at A and B (figure 18) so that an equal amount of fabric lies on either side of the pins.

3. Smooth the fabric outwards towards the struts P-Q and S-T, placing temporary pins at both ends of these struts. Working from the centre of these, pin and gradually ease away the fullness.

4. Pin along the top and bottom rings, easing away the fullness.

5. Stitch around this section with Streatley stitch. Roll back the surplus fabric along the struts and secure as in figure 17. Trim very neatly.

6. If the cover or lining is made in four separate sections, next fit and attach the section opposite the first and then the two intervening sections. It will not be necessary to roll back and neaten the raw edges of the last two sections as the raw edges of these will be neatened by the trimmings. This also applies to the second half of the shade if the cover or lining is attached in two pieces.

7. To neaten the struts to which you have stitched the fabric, cut two or four crossway strips of the fabric 2·5 cm (1 in) wide and iron the raw edges towards the centre of the strip. The strips should be slightly longer than the struts themselves. Attach one end of one strip to the top ring to cover the raw edge of the panel. Bring the strip down to the bottom ring and tighten. Because it is on the cross it will stretch around the convex curve and grip the frame, so making it unnecessary to stitch along the strut. Secure to the lower ring.

8. Roll back the fabric along the lower ring and stitch. Trim away

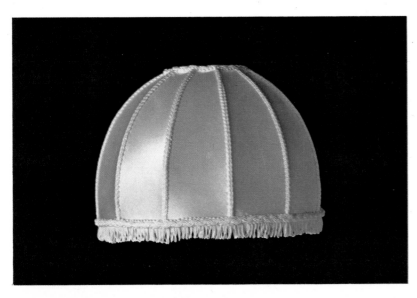

Three Tiffany shades covered in different ways

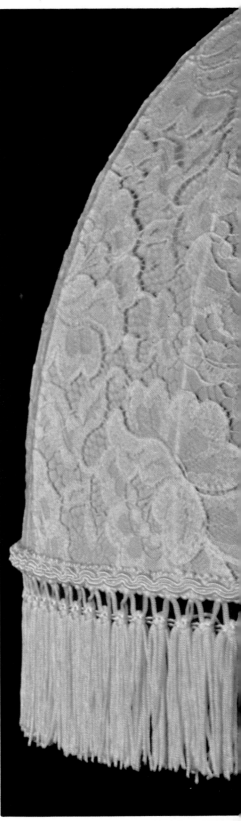

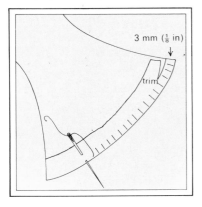

17 *Finishing the edge of cover*

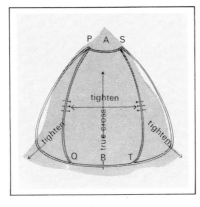

18 *Fitting a Tiffany tailored shade*

any excess fabric from both rings.
Note Do not roll the fabric along the top ring.

Drum Shade with Tailored Lining and Pleated Cover

For a frame of this type with a diameter of 25 cm (10 in) or less you will need approximately 0·3 m ($\frac{1}{4}$ yd) of lining fabric, 0·75 m ($\frac{3}{4}$ yd) of chiffon for a cover with touching pleats, or 0·5 m ($\frac{1}{2}$ yd) of chiffon for spaced pleats, and tape for binding the rings.

Begin by painting the frame to match the lining in the usual way. Then bind the rings and struts. If making a cover with spaced pleats, bind the struts with ribbon to match the lining.

Fitting the lining

1. Divide the lining into two equal pieces, each measuring 25 x 45 cm (9 x 18 in). Place one piece over half the frame. Insert temporary pins at the top and bottom of two opposite struts.
2. Pin the lining to the top ring at point X. Tighten towards the bottom ring and insert a pin at Y. Work outwards from these two points towards the two struts A-B and C-D, tightening vertically all the time (figure 19).
3. Pin down the two struts without pulling horizontally.

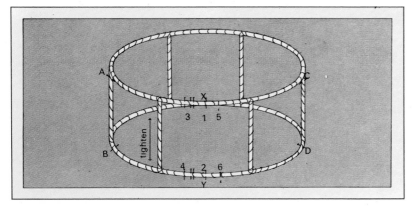

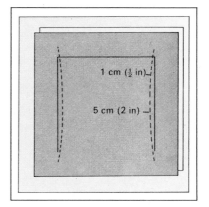

19 Fitting lining for drum shade

20 Fitting and assembling lining for drum

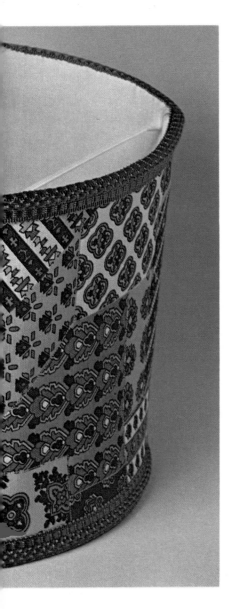

4. Mark the outline of the top ring and two struts, then trim to 1 cm ($\frac{1}{2}$ in) at the sides and 5 cm (2 in) at the top and bottom.

5. Place the marked pattern on the second half of the fabric. Pin along the pencilled lines and draw the reduced fitting line (figure 20).

6. Tack along these lines and test the lining for fit. If the lining appears to fit perfectly, it will eventually prove to be too large and fullness will develop on the rings. It should therefore be slightly tight fitting. When you are happy with the size, stitch the side seams and tailor tack the line of the top ring.

Note Fit a tailored cover for a drum shade in the same way, but stitch the side seams along the pencilled lines making no reductions. Do not insert the lining.

Fitting the pleated cover

7. Begin by deciding on the depth of the pleats. 1 cm ($\frac{1}{2}$ in) is about right on a smaller shade and you should increase the depth of the pleat proportionally on larger frames. Many drums are tapered, i.e. the diameter of the top ring is a little less than that of the lower ring. As a result, the pleats will be a little closer together on the top ring.

8. Mark the binding on the lower ring every 1 cm ($\frac{1}{2}$ in) or the depth decided upon for each pleat.

Quilted, Terylene–wadded shade

9. Tear a strip of chiffon equal to the depth of the shade, plus 3 cm (1 in).

10. Turn in by 1 cm ($\frac{1}{2}$ in) and place the strip over a strut (figure 21). Pin at A and B.

11. Then pin the chiffon to the lower ring 2 cm ($\frac{3}{4}$ in) from the front edge of the formed pleat (figure 22).

12. Fold back the chiffon by 1 cm ($\frac{1}{2}$ in) so that it just overlaps the first pleat and pin. Complete the pinning along the lower ring to the next strut (figure 23).

13. Return to the second pleat and fold the chiffon along the grain, anchoring it to the top ring. If the drum is a true drum, this pleat will be 1 cm ($\frac{1}{2}$ in) from the first pleat; slightly less with a tapered drum. Check that all the pleats are at right angles to the lower ring. When working on a true drum, the top and bottom of each pleat can be completed at the same time but when working on a tapered drum it is easier to work one panel at a time.

14. Continue pleating until you reach the end of the first piece of chiffon, finishing as described in stage 11. Tear or trim away any slight excess of chiffon.

15. Stitch the fabric to the bottom ring, then to the top ring, tightening each pleat as it is secured. Leave the first pleat unstitched.

16. To join the fabric, fold under 1 cm ($\frac{1}{2}$ in) at the beginning of the

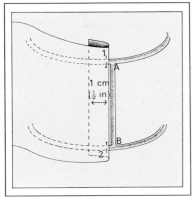

21 Touching pleats on true drum

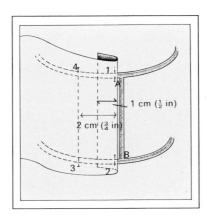

22 Touching pleats, stage two

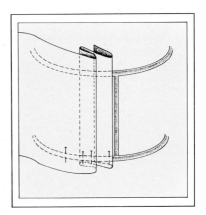

23 Touching pleats, stage three

second piece of chiffon and place it over the end of the last strip to give a continuous pleating.

17. Finish by inserting the last 1 cm ($\frac{1}{2}$ in) of the last pleat under the first pleat so that the pleats are unbroken right around the frame.

18. On the rings, trim the fabric right back to the stitching.

19. Insert the lining and stitch into position. Work the stitches on the outside of the rings so that they will be hidden by the trimmings.

Shade with Twin-colour Pleating

This is a more extravagant method of pleating but one which is very popular and most effective. The pleats fan out from points on the top and bottom rings to give alternate triangles of light and dark pleating. Use the lighter-toned fabric at the top of the shade or the finished effect will be top-heavy. It is essential to use a very sheer fabric as this form of pleating results in considerable bulk at the points from which the pleats fan out. Chiffon and georgette are the most suitable.

Measuring the fabrics

For the lighter-coloured fabric, measure the length of one strut and then add 5 cm (2 in) for the depth

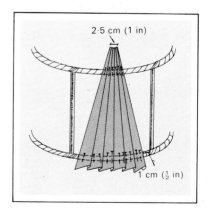

24 Twin-pleated shade

of each strip of fabric. Measure the circumference of the top ring and multiply this by three. Depending on the width of the fabric, you can then calculate the number of strips you will need—usually two or three for small- to medium-sized shades. For the darker colour, make the same calculation but measure the circumference of the lower ring. You will find that you need an extra one or two strips of this colour.

Preparing the frame

Prepare the frame in the usual way but bind the struts with ribbon to match the colour of the lining.

Preparing the lining

Fit and cut the lining as for a bowed empire shade but do not fit before attaching the cover.

Pleating the shade

1. Take the paler fabric and divide it into six or eight equal pieces, depending on the number of struts to the frame. Each will be the height of the frame plus a working allowance of 5 cm (2 in).
2. Divide the darker fabric in the same way.
3. Using the darker fabric, start pleating on the lower ring 1 cm ($\frac{1}{2}$ in) from one strut. Pleat as for the pleated drum along one section of

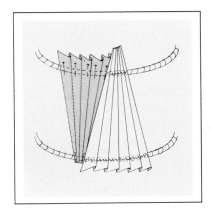

25 Fan-pleated shade

this ring but do not attach the top edge of the strip. Finish the last pleat 1 cm ($\frac{1}{2}$ in) from the second strut but extend a single thickness of the fabric to this strut before tearing away any excess (figure 24).
4. Mark halfway along the section of the top ring above that to which the chiffon is attached. Mark 1 cm ($\frac{1}{4}$ in) either side of this point. Returning to the first pleat on the bottom ring, fold the fabric along the grain and stretch up to the top ring, pinning to the right hand marking.
5. Repeat with each pleat but anchor them all within the 2-cm (1-in) space in the central section of the top ring, except where the single layer of chiffon lies under the next triangle of pleats.
6. Stitch these pleats into position but leave the first pleats unstitched for 1 cm ($\frac{1}{2}$ in) to allow for finishing and neatening.
7. Take one of the lighter strips of

fabric and begin pleating this along the top ring. The first pleat will cover the single layer of chiffon at the end of the previous set of pleats. Continue to within 1 cm ($\frac{1}{2}$ in) of the halfway point of the next panel. This set of pleats will be to the left of that already attached.
8. Extend the pleats down to the bottom ring and fit them into the space 1 cm ($\frac{1}{2}$ in) each side of the strut (figure 25).
9. Continue to attach alternate fans of light and dark pleats until the cover is complete. Fit the end of the last set of light-coloured pleats under the first pleat of the first set of dark pleats (figures 24, 25). Trim away all surplus fabric and complete as for the pleated drum shade.
Note A combination of narrow velvet ribbon with a metallic lace makes a very elegant trimming

(Left) Bowed empire, tailored cover
(Above) Fan-pleated shade

(Above) Square bowed shade, the cover was fitted in four panels and trimmed with matching coloured braid (Left and previous page) Fan-pleated shades; you can clearly see overleaf the spaced pleats at the wide end of the fan, they overlap at the apex. Note the trimming braid at the top and matching bobble edging at the bottom in complementary colours: the shades on the left have been built up on fluted rings that give a pleasant scalloped shape which is set off by the fan pleating.

Square Bowed Shade with Four Panels

This is a very economical shade as it can be made up from remnants. If two patterned panels are used with two plain, the results can look most attractive, especially if the plain panels pick up one of the colours in the patterned panels. Here you will have no colour conflict in the choice of trimming as you will have a range of complementary colours. Bind both rings and the four struts of the frame with tape.

Making the lining

1. Cut this in four sections, noting that you will have to take a little more care than when working with two sections. Machine the panels together to form a tube.

Preparing the cover

2. Lay the frame flat on the table and place the lining *right* side uppermost, over one of the four sections. Check that the grain of the lining fabric runs from the centre of the top of the panel to the centre of the bottom of the panel (figure 26).

3. Fit on the straight of the grain or thread as for the tailored lining (refer back to figure 13). You may need to tighten the fabric a little vertically.

4. Take a pencil and mark lightly on the inside of the shade, marking the inside of the frame also (figure 27).

5. Cut four identical panels, marking each one accurately.

6. Mark the stitching lines on both sides of each panel; no reductions are necessary at the top and bottom of the seams (figure 28). Curve the lines inwards 1 cm ($\frac{1}{2}$ in) in the centre of each seam to allow for the bowing away from the frame that always occurs. Check the fit before inserting and stitching, as in figure 28, which shows the stitching line curved in 1 cm ($\frac{1}{2}$ in) at the seam centre, from the right side.

Fitting the cover

7. Fit one panel as for the lining but stitch directly to the bound struts. Fit the panel directly opposite and then the remaining two. Keep the stitches on the strut as small as possible to avoid the need for a wide trimming.

8. Roll back and neaten the fabric at the top and bottom of the shade. Trim the struts, then the rings. A braid-type trimming is preferable to fringing and tassels, which are rather too fussy for this style of shade.

> *The dyes in some commercial trimmings are not fast. Bear this in mind if you plan to use dark braids on pale covers.*
>
> *Make sure that your cover fits on the struts before beginning to stitch it.*
>
> *Be careful not to stretch lace too tightly when fitting the cover, or it may lift away from the external lining.*

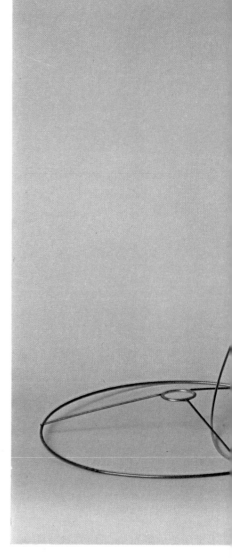

Drum shade made from tie-dyed lawn on selapar producing a firm cover; wire rings, as shown on the left, can be used in making drum shades from various firm materials, instead of making shades from frames with struts; note that the pendant fitting should be recessed and go at the top for a hanging shade and at the bottom for a reading lampshade

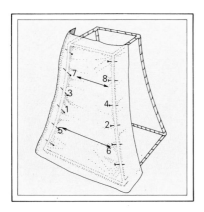

26 Tailored lining for square shade

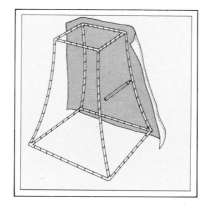

27 Square shade, marking the lining

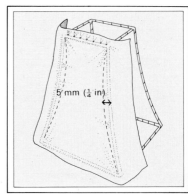

28 Square shade, marking stitching line

Drum Shade from Firm Material

This style needs two rings, one plain and another with a suitable fitting. You will also require a rectangle of material, the depth of which is equal to the height of the finished shade and the length equal to the circumference of the rings plus 1 cm ($\frac{1}{2}$ in) for an overlap. Bind the rings to match the inside colour of the firm material (usually white).

Preparing the cover

1. Cut out the cover, using a Stanley knife against a metal ruler. This ensures clear-cut edges. Many of the firm materials available are bonded with fabric, so avoid any white showing on the overlap. To do this, allow an extra 3 mm ($\frac{1}{8}$ in) on the overlap and cut away this width of the backing card.
2. Lift the surface fabric or material from the backing by running a needle down between the two layers. Take care, however, not to cut the top material when removing the card.
3. Fold back the extra material and stick down with a little adhesive applied with a pin. This edge forms the top edge at the join.

Assembling the shade

4. Using clothes pegs or alligator clips, fit the material around one ring, the top of the material being just level with the top of the ring (figure 29).
5. Stitch the material to the ring using running or Streatley stitch.
6. Attach the second ring in the same way. If using a recessed pendant fitting, the fitting should be inside the shade.
7. To join the overlap, use a clear adhesive such as clear Bostik and apply with a pin to the upper surface of the overlap. This avoids a soiled join.

Choose a warm, dry, breezy day to wash your stitched lampshades. Turn them upside down where possible to prevent water lines forming as the shades dry. Try to dry them as quickly as you can (but certainly not in any heated cabinet). Too much heat applied too quickly will cause the metal frame to expand, which, upon cooling and contracting, will cause the cover to be loose and slack. A glued shade can only be cleaned by washing.

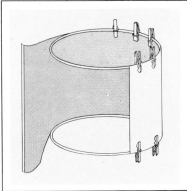

29 Fitting a firm drum cover

8. Trim as simply as possible for the best effect.

Cone Shade

You will have to draw a graph to make a cover for this style of shade. This is not difficult but it must be accurate. Graph paper is generally available from most good stationers.

A cone shade requires two rings, one with a suitable fitting, plus firm material for the cover (but do not buy this until you have drawn the graph). You will also need binding for the rings and trimming for the finished shade.

Making a graph

Decide on the height of the finished shade, then measure the diameter of both rings (figure 30).

1. Draw a line A-B equal to the diameter of the lower ring.
2. Mark the mid-point of this line S-M, then draw a line through M at right angles to A-B. This *must* be accurate.
3. Mark off the height of the shade M-T—this is a vertical line. (This is *not* the length of the sloping side of the shade.)
4. Draw a horizontal line through T parallel to A-B and mark it C-D. C-D is equal to the diameter of the smaller ring, T being the mid-point of C-D.
5. Join A-D and continue this line

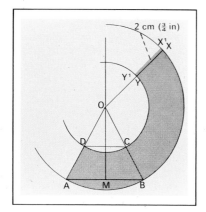

30 Graph for cone shade

until it cuts M-T extended at O.
6. Cheek that B-C passes through O when continued. If this does not occur, check your work.
7. With radius O-A and centre O, draw an arc which passes through B.
8. With radius O-D and centre O draw an arc which passes through C.
9. Beginning at A, roll the large ring carefully around the arc A-B (extended) and mark X. The lower edge of the ring must roll along the arc. A-X measures the circumference of the large ring.
10. Check this measurement by repeating the rolling of the ring.
11. Join X to O, cutting the inner arc at Y.
12. Mark the overlap allowance of 6 mm ($\frac{1}{4}$ in) as Y′X′. Cut out the shaded section. When making up this shade, always cut the pattern first in strong paper and test by fitting to the rings. Draw the large arcs with the aid of a strip of cardboard 1 cm ($\frac{1}{2}$ in) wide. Anchor it at O with a drawing-pin and pivot around this point.

Making the shade

13. The pattern must be placed on the material with care if any fabric has been bonded on to a backing. The centre line of the paper pattern must match the grain of the fabric. On the completed shade, the straight of the grain will run diametrically opposite the overlap and so give a balanced appearance to the shade.
14. Cut out the pattern, making sure you have a smooth edge. Fix the outer edge of the material to the larger ring, holding it in position with pegs. The resistance of the stiff material to curving round the ring would force pins out of position.
15. Stitch with running stitches or Streatley stitch. Begin stitching about 2 cm ($\frac{3}{4}$ in) away from the overlap and, working away from the overlap, stitch round the ring and finally work over the join. By leaving this to the end of the stitching, you will avoid any fullness.

16. Place the shade on a flat surface to test for an even base. Then fix and attach the top ring in the same way.

Working the join

17. Keep this neat and clean. The taller the shade, the more care you should give to the join. Spread a piece of clean polythene or plastic on a table before beginning to stick the join.

Spread a thin layer of adhesive underneath the upper piece of the overlap. Place the shade with the join on the polythene, then insert a second piece of polythene over the join inside the shade. Place a weight over the join, preferably an article which covers the whole of the length of the join. This will prevent any bulges developing in the seam while it is drying.
18. Trim with a braid-type edging.

Collared bowed empire shade with tailored cover of patterned fabric requiring closely matched joins. This collar is at the base of the shade and has been finished with matching ribbon and an attractive double tassel border picking up the colours of the fabric

> ### Hints
> *You can indulge in more expensive tastes when buying fabrics for lampshades because the quantities required are generally small.*
>
> *Time spent on preparing the frame will be time saved, as the shade is likely to keep its taut shape and crisp appearance for much longer on a well-prepared frame.*
>
> *Always use the smallest pins you can find for the job—they make the smallest holes in the fabric, and in your fingers.*
>
> *If blood gets on to your fabric while you are pinning up your shade cover, wash the fabric before attaching.*

Trimmings

The shade's trimming will decide its finished effect, so choose something suitable and attach it with care. The choice of a trimming is of course a personal one, but remember that it should complete and complement rather than dominate the finished shade.

There is a wide choice of commercially produced trimmings, many of them expensive. In fact, it is possible for a trimming to cost more than the rest of the shade.

There is much to recommend making your own trimmings, but they must be done well and co-ordinate with the shade in question. This is an area where you can experiment and have a lot of fun in achieving an original result.

If using a fabric that requires a second craft, such as pulled-thread embroidery, machine embroidery, bobbin lace or tatting, etc., make every effort to make a matching edging. This will not only improve the appearance of the shade but add considerably to its value as an original piece of craftwork.

Attaching trimmings

On soft fabric shades, trimmings must be stitched and not glued in place. This ensures that they will not become detached when the shade is washed or cleaned, nor will there be any danger of the adhesive yellowing and so marking the fabric.

Since most firm shades cannot be washed, you can stick trimmings in place with complete safety. Use a suitable clear adhesive and one which will not yellow with age. Apply it sparingly, and *not* directly from the tube, which may drip. A thick needle makes an excellent applicator.

When stitching a trimming into position, use herringbone stitch (refer back to figure 9). Seal any ends of trimmings which are likely to fray with a little adhesive before cutting. All forms of trimmings are there to neaten raw edges and cover the last row of stitching, so they must be chosen or made sufficiently wide to achieve this aim.

Stretch braid-type trimmings into position so that they curve over the rings. Do not stretch fringes or bobble edgings in this way or the hanging threads will fall from inside the lower ring of the shade.

Rectangular bowed shade with cover of pulled linen embroidery worked on an open-weave scrim; the self-colour base binding is of scrim and the light-weight tassels that form the trimming are made from the scrim threads. The shade is shown with the gimbal fitting bent to show embroidery design

---

Hints

Fabric required for shades:
   Tailored, diameter 40 cm (12 in), requires 0·3–0·5 m ($\frac{1}{3}$–$\frac{1}{2}$ yd) of fabric for cover or lining.
   Shade, diameter 50 cm (20 in), requires 1 m (1 yd) of fabric for cover or lining.
   Shade, diameter 60 cm (24 in), requires 1·2 m (1$\frac{1}{4}$ yd) of fabric for cover or lining.
   Measure diameter of lower ring for all above shades.
   On the two rings of a frame match the joins of trimmings so that they coincide over the seam.
   Try to match any patterned braid for a continuous line.
   To prevent trimmings fraying, treat the ends with a little adhesive before cutting.
   In choosing your trimmings bear in mind not only colour and texture but also width. The trimming is there to neaten raw edges— have it sufficiently wide.

Lampshade materials suppliers

Avon	Home Accessories 35 Park St BRISTOL
Berks.	Caleys High St WINDSOR
	Heelas Broad St READING
Cambs.	Robert Sayle St Andrews St CAMBRIDGE
Cumb.	Merricrafts 9 Lowther St CARLISLE
Derby	Arts & Crafts Green Lane DERBY
	U-do-it Church St RIPLEY
Essex	A. J. Franklin 58 Head St. COLCHESTER
Glos.	Elscott Interior Design 23 Imperial Sq CHELTENHAM
	Dorothy Pye High St MORETON-IN-MARSH
Hants.	Knight & Lee Palmerston Rd SOUTHSEA
Kent	Handicraft Shop 47 Northgate CANTERBURY
Lancs.	George Henry Lee Basnett St LIVERPOOL
	Russell Trading Co. 75 Paradise St LIVERPOOL
Leics.	Yvonne & Co. 17 King St LEICESTER
	Yvonne & Co. 5 High St UPPINGHAM
London	John Barnes Finchley Rd NW3
	Distinctive Trimmings
	17D Kensington Church St W8
	Distinctive Trimmings
	11 Marylebone Lane W1
	Jones Brothers Holloway Rd N7
	Peter Jones Sloane Sq SW1
	Lampshade Supply Service
	21 Jordan Pl SW6
	John Lewis Brent Cross Shopping Centre NW4
	John Lewis Oxford St W1
	Pratts Streatham High Rd SW16
	Trewin Brothers Queen's Rd WATFORD
Northumb.	Bainbridge Eldon Sq NEWCASTLE-UPON-TYNE
Notts.	Jessop & Son Victoria Centre NOTTINGHAM
Oxon.	R. J. Hughes 60 North St THAME
Somerset	Spinning Wheel 22 Billett St TAUNTON

Staffs.	Midland Educational 24 Wulfrun Way WOLVERHAMPTON
Surrey	L. H. Turtle 10 Park St CROYDON
Sussex	Handicrafts 6 Circus Parade Preston Circus BRIGHTON
Warwicks.	Shadecrafts 4 Park St LEAMINGTON SPA
Wilts.	Mace & Nairn 89 Crane St SALISBURY
Yorks.	Cole Brothers Barkers Pool SHEFFIELD
Scotland	
Lothian	John Lewis St James Centre EDINBURGH

Books for further reference

Modern Lampshade Book, Dorothy Cox, Bell & Hyman, 1973

Lampshade Making, Lucie Dickson, Arco, 1964

Making Lampshades, Dryad Handicrafts, Dryad, fourth edition, 1968

Lampshade Technique and Design, Angela Fishburn, Batsford, 1974

Lampshades: Simple and Advanced, Margaret Rourke, Mills & Boon, 1969

Lampshade Making, Phyllis Sharples, Bell & Hyman, 1966

Upholstery materials suppliers   * Fabrics and trimmings only   † Wholesalers only—contact for foam retail outlets

This list of suppliers is offered merely as an aid to purchasers. It is not comprehensive, but to the publishers' knowledge the details are correct at the time of publishing. WI Books Ltd and the publishers cannot accept responsibility for the accuracy of the information.

Avon	Brunswick Furnishing Fabrics Wilson St BRISTOL
Beds.	S. Hodgson 36 High St SHEFFORD
	Jacks Ltd. 15-16 Westside Centre LUTON
	McClaren & Dunlop 69 Tavistock St BEDFORD
	F E Puleston 148 Leagrave Rd LUTON
	W. J. West 42-58 King St POTTON
Berks.	*Caleys High St WINDSOR
	*Heelas Broad St READING
Bucks.	Kash 'n' Karry 6 The Concourse MILTON KEYNES
Cambs.	* Robert Sayle St Andrews St CAMBRIDGE
Derby	U-do-it Church St RIPLEY
Co. Durham	Ideal Upholsterers 191 Northgate DARLINGTON
Essex	Barkingside DIY Centre Ltd. 104 High St BARKINGSIDE
	L. W. Chesney 21 West Rd WESTCLIFF-ON-SEA
	K. W. Clark Foams 138 Southchurch Ave SOUTHEND
	Gem Upholsterers 157 Southend Rd GRAYS
	J. E. James 32 Clarendon Rd GRAYS
	A. Prickett & Sons 138 Broadway LEIGH ON SEA
	Strand Upholsterers 793 Southchurch Rd SOUTHEND
	F. W. Tuck & Son Industrial B'dgs Beehive Lane CHELMSFORD
Glos.	Cavendish House The Parade CHELTENHAM
Hants.	J. Small 88 Dean Rd BITTERNE
	Fine Fabrics (Alton) The Post House High St ALTON
	Fireside Chairs 259 Holdenhurst Rd BOURNEMOUTH
	*Knight & Lee Palmerston Rd SOUTHSEA
	Trimfabs 299 Shirley Rd SOUTHAMPTON
Kent	Bonners of Welling 35 Upper Wickham Lane WELLING
	Do-It-Yourself Centre 59 High St BECKENHAM

	Fourways Furniture Fourways Corner Cross Rd BOROUGH GREEN
	J. P. Shearn 9 Park Place DOVER
Lancs.	*George Henry Lee Basnett St LIVERPOOL
	H. A. Nicholson 75 Wigan Lane WIGAN
	Russell Trading Co. 75 Paradise St LIVERPOOL
	†John Singleton North St MANCHESTER 8
Leics.	Auto Trim Wesley St LEICESTER
	†George Danby 12 Sanvey Gate LEICESTER
	Ryte Lynes Upholstery Co 4 Shaftesbury Rd LEICESTER
Lincs.	Clayton Upholsterers 26-28 Portland St LINCOLN
Norfolk	Fishers 170 High St LOWESTOFT
	Taskers of Fishergate Fishergate NORWICH
Northants.	S. A. Craxton 295 Wellingborough Rd NORTHAMPTON
	Cygnet Soft Furnishings 7 St Leonards Rd FAR COTTON
Northumb.	*Bainbridge Eldon Sq NEWCASTLE-UPON-TYNE
	Wadecraft Carliol Sq NEWCASTLE-UPON-TYNE
Notts.	*Jessop & Son Victoria Centre NOTTINGHAM
	R Mould 123 Mansfield Rd DAYBROOK
Suffolk	Howgego 19-21 Fore St IPSWICH
Surrey	Emjay Camping Supplies 595 London Rd NORTH CHEAM
	R. J. F. Upholstery 101 Stoke Rd GUILDFORD
	Gatestone 8 Carshalton Pk Rd CARSHALTON
	B & M Latex Sales 73 Station Rd ADDLESTON
Sussex	W. J. O'Brien Southcourt Rd WORTHING
	Price & Co 87 St George's Rd BRIGHTON
Worcs.	Worcestershire Rubber & Belting Co. 43 The Tything WORCESTER

Yorks.	Chadd Upholsterers 10 Sandygate Rd Crosspool SHEFFIELD ∗ Cole Brothers Barkers Pool SHEFFIELD Doncaster Upholsterers 19 Hexthorpe Rd DONCASTER Foam for Comfort East Bush Lane OTLEY Gibbons Upholstery 9 Netherhall Rd DONCASTER Local Trading 207 London Rd SHEFFIELD M. B. Smith 58 Clarence St YORK Spa Foam Melbourne St LEEDS
Wales **Carnarvon** **Glam.**	Jackson & Ashworth Farrar Rd Gwynedd BANGOR Carrefour Pontygwindy Rd CAERPHILLY Cohen & Pontin 81 Bridge St CARDIFF L. L. Davies 426 Cowbridge Rd East CARDIFF A. J. Roberts 8 Tudor Rd CARDIFF
Gwent	Superease Upholsterers 5 Hannah St Porth RHONDDA D. & B. Thorne Friars St NEWPORT I. R. Taylor 12 Malpas Rd NEWPORT
Scotland **Fife** **Grampian** **Lothian** **Strathclyde**	Markinch Co-op Balbourne St MARKINCH Chas. K. Davie 13–15 Thistle Pl ABERDEEN ∗ John Lewis St James Centre EDINBURGH Richard Wylie 48A Hamilton Pl STOCKBRIDGE Jacksons Upholstery Supplies 368 Argyle St GLASGOW 2 James Love & Sons Avon St LARKHALL Currie Thompson 45 Jamaica St GLASGOW 1 Timberland 125 Main St COATBRIDGE

Glossary

alligator clips	clips that can be used instead of pegs for holding firm fabric to the rings in a lampshade frame
balloon lining	a lining fitted inside the struts of the frame and usually consisting of two or four sections
bevelled	with the sharp edges removed (usually refers to wood)
bias	across the grain, i.e., in fabric, not on the straight of the thread, the line of the bias runs midway between the warp and weft threads
bowed empire lampshade	a shade in which the two rings are separated by struts which are bowed or bent in a concave curve
box pleats	pleats that stand out on the right side of the material with the two edges of one pleat facing in opposite directions
bridles	lengths of twine stitched into hessian or anchored to a wooden base by tacks, under which stuffing is placed
butt join	point at which two edges meet edge to edge but do not overlap
butterfly clip	a form of fitment used on candle shades; two rings with a butterfly appearance clip on to an upright bulb
calico	a cotton fabric with an even weave; in its natural state it is ecru in colour
cambric	a very finely woven cotton fabric, frequently treated or proofed to prevent feathers or down escaping and one side may be glossy or glazed
chiffon	a sheer fabric made from silk or man-made fibres; it is suitable for swathing, gathering or pleating on lampshades
coir	a vegetable fibre used in upholstery
countersink	to remove a layer of wood so that the top of a screw is lower than the surface of the wood
crepe	a gauzelike fabric with a crinkled surface
curtain track	metal or plastic rail, attached to the wall or ceiling, from which curtains are suspended
cut on the bias	cut on a line halfway between the warp and weft threads
cut on the true cross	cut on a line halfway between the warp and weft threads. This line gives maximum stretch. Material cut in strips on the true cross is used

cut on the straight	for covering piping cord as a sleeve.
	the line of the warp and weft threads passes down the centre of a panel (lampshades)
doming	extra stuffing or foam introduced to give upholstery a domed or curved shape
Dralon	a man-made fibre used in the manufacture of fabrics used in upholstery or soft furnishing
drum shade	a lampshade frame resembling a drum in shape; the upper and lower rings may have the same diameter; alternatively, the top ring may be slightly smaller
dupion	a furnishing fabric in which the weft thread may vary in thickness producing an unusual texture
duvet	a form of bedcover developed from the continental bedcover; it overhangs the mattress, is filled with down or man-made fibre, and can be used on its own or with a sheet
fan pleats	a group of pleats radiating from a restricted area and spreading out in the form of a fan
feathering	cutting away a portion of the depth of foam to give a gradual rise to finished upholstery
georgette	a sheer fabric similar to chiffon
gimbal fitting	a small ring attached to the top ring of a shade by two long arms which are usually hinged, it is used on reading-lamp shades
gimp	a type of braid used in upholstery; it usually has S-shaped loops passing from edge to edge, which may be lifted for inserting gimp pins to attach the gimp to the frame; the pins are hidden when the loops are lowered
gimp pins	fine upholstery tacks, available in a variety of colours, which are used to attach gimp
gusset	usually referred to as a 'box' in soft furnishing: a strip of material, cut on the straight, which separates the upper and lower sections of a cushion; it may be used to produce a square edge in upholstery
heading	the top edge of a curtain and the means by which the curtain is hung
herringbone	a sewing stitch with the appearance of two rows of detached stitches,

	used to attach lampshade braids
hessian	a coarse, heavy jute fabric used in upholstery
kapok	a kind of tree-cotton used to stuff cushions; not recommended as it tends to go lumpy
knife pleats	narrow parallel pleats, the edges of which all face in the same direction
Lillikin pins ('Lills')	very tiny plated pins used in lampshade-making
lining sateen	a strong, closely woven, cotton fabric with a satin weave and shiny finish; it is used for lining curtains and backing bedheads and is available in a variety of colours
mercerized cotton	cotton thread treated to give a glossy or glazed surface
Paris binding	a narrow fabric similar to tape, made with an even or twill weave in cotton, silk or man-made fibre and available in a variety of colours
pelmet	a decorative border attached to wall or ceiling to obscure curtain fittings; usually made of wood, hardboard or buckram, pelmets may either be covered with material or painted
pencil pleats	very fine pleats, usually knife pleats
pinch pleats	form of pleating often used for curtain headings; normally arranged in groups of three pleats separated by unpleated areas
Pirelli webbing	a rubberized webbing, the rubber being imposed on strips of material that have been cut on the bias
piping	a decorative edging, comprising a cord of cotton or nylon covered by crossway strips of matching or contrasting fabric; cotton cord must be pre-shrunk
piping foot	see zipper foot
plastic wood	a commercial material which among other uses can be used to fill holes left by tacks during stripping
quilt	a bedcover, usually consisting of two layers of material joined to form a bag which is filled with down, down/feather mixture, synthetic fibre or sheep's wool. The two layers are stitched or quilted together to hold the filling in place
rebate	a layer of wood inside and below the surface of the main area of a piece of furniture, on which a loose frame may sit on webbing attached

regulator	an upholstery tool, made of steel; the pointed end can be inserted through scrim to regulate the filling during stitching up
rouleau	a tube of crossway material
ruching	a gathered frill of double material; a cord may be threaded through the frill to give a ruched piping
selapar	a firm fabric used to make lampshades; one side has a waxed cover which can be removed so that a soft fabric may be applied
selvedge	the edge of a woven fabric, usually the warp threads are doubled on the selvedge to a depth of approximately 1 cm ($\frac{1}{2}$ in)
scrim	a lightweight open-weave fabric; when made of jute it is used to cover the first stuffing in traditional upholstery
scroll gimp	see gimp
sheer nets	very fine nets; when used as curtains they give privacy without excluding any appreciable amount of light
slip-hemming	a method of stitching the hem of a curtain invisibly; only a thread of the back surface of the top material is picked up in each stitch
spaced pleats	a series of pleats where a space of single fabric is left between adjacent pleats
squab cushion	a form of box cushion firmly stuffed; used on dining chairs
Stanley knife	a knife with retractable sharp blade used for cutting cord or trimming fabric
Streatley stitch	a secure stitch used to attach fabrics to lampshade frames; also used in glove-making
swathes	fullness taken from the bottom ring of a lampshade diagonally to the top ring
swing-needle machine	a sewing machine designed so that the needle can move from side to side to produce a zig-zag stitch
tack-draws	shadowy line running from a tack into the material; usually due to incorrect or over-tightening
tailor tacks	detached loose back stitches worked on double fabric with loops of thread between adjacent stitches; after stitching, the two layers are opened and the threads passing

	between the layers are snipped
Terylene floss	a man-made fibre teased out to resemble candy-floss; it is used for filling cushions and duvets
tussore	a silk fabric of unusual texture; imitations are now made from synthetic threads
Tiffany shade	a lampshade style resembling an inverted tulip
upholstery adhesive	a specially designed adhesive which will unite foam to calico to give a strong join and yet remain flexible
valance	a frill around a bedbase, usually below the mattress and falling to the floor; valances may be plain, gathered or pleated
Velcro	a commercial product for fastenings, useful in cushion-making; it is made in two sections: one portion has a velvet finish, the other a hooked surface and the two sections adhere when pressed together
to web	to attach webbing to the frame of a piece of furniture
web stretcher	a tool used to attach webbing to the frame of a piece of furniture
welt	see gusset
Wonderweb	a commercial product for securing hems in position
zipper foot	a half foot which can be attached to a sewing machine to permit stitching close to a zip or piping, usually but not always identical to a piping foot; designs vary according to the make of machine

Index

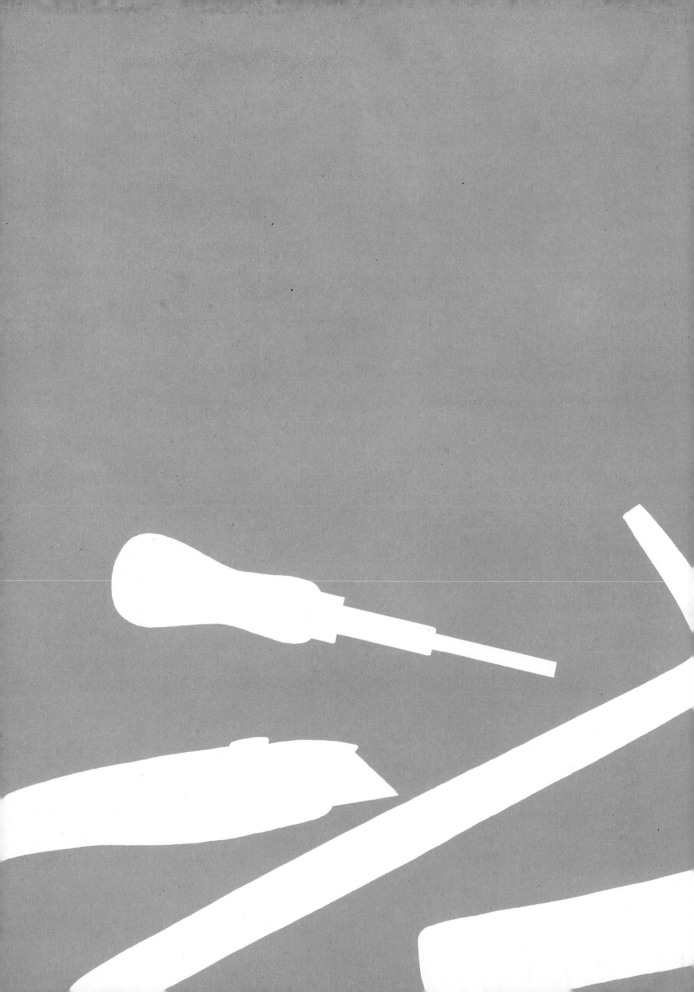